1 MONTH OF
FREE
READING

at

www.ForgottenBooks.com

By purchasing this book you are
eligible for one month membership to
ForgottenBooks.com, giving you
unlimited access to our entire
collection of over 1,000,000 titles via
our web site and mobile apps.

To claim your free month visit:

www.forgottenbooks.com/free783745

ISBN 978-0-428-94760-6
PIBN 10783745

This book is a reproduction of an important historical work. Forgotten Books uses state-of-the-art technology to digitally reconstruct the work, preserving the original format whilst repairing imperfections present in the aged copy. In rare cases, an imperfection in the original, such as a blemish or missing page, may be replicated in our edition. We do, however, repair the vast majority of imperfections successfully; any imperfections that remain are intentionally left to preserve the state of such historical works.

A HART SCHAFFNER & MARX
NORFOLK—IT HAS STYLE

YOU probably say it often—a certain man "has style" You aren't thinking of the details of his clothes as much as his whole bearing and manner Our clothes are that way—they "have style"; not in the lines alone, but in the total effect; the all-wool fabrics, fine quality, expert needlework and all

Find our label—and you'll have the style you want

HART SCHAFFNER & MARX

Official publication of
The American Legion
and The American
Legion Auxiliary.

Published by the Le-
gion Publishing Corp.:
President, Alvin Ows-
ley; Vice-President,
James A. Drain; Treas-
urer, Robert H. Tyn-
dall; Secretary, Lemuel
Bolles.

The AMERICAN LEGION Weekly

BUSINESS OFFICE
(Advertising and Circulation)
627 West 43d Street, New York City

EDITORIAL OFFICES
Natl. Hqtrs. Bureau, Indianapolis, Ind.
627 W. 43d St., New York City

Owned exclusively by
The American Legion.

Correspondence and
manuscripts pertaining
to Legion activities
should be addressed to
the National Head-
quarters Bureau. All
other communications
should be addressed to
the New York office.

A Sequel to "Who Got the Money?"

The Profiteer Hunt

V. Sought from Two Contractors—$3,500,000

By Marquis James

The Evidence in the Government's Case Against the American Electro Products Company and the Duesenberg Motors Corporation—The Trail Crosses an International Boundary

OUR discussion has progressed to a phase wherein the Weekly is able to identify by name certain contractors who have been sighted as quarry in the profiteer hunt. Investigation of their affairs by official agencies has reached a point where action toward a settlement either in or out of the courts seems assured. This situation, furthermore, enables this magazine to present certain features of the Government's case against some of these contractors—features which may now be disclosed without prejudice to the public interest.

We have at hand the case of the American Electro Products Company, a Canadian concern, of Shawinigan Falls, Quebec. The agreement this corporation received from the United States Government was one of the most surprising contracts written during the war. And the circumstances under which the contract was obtained by (or thrust upon) this company are equally astonishing.

The peculiar nature of this transaction became apparent long before there was any thought of a general investigation of war contracts. In 1920 the matter was called to the attention of Newton D. Baker, then Secretary of War. He asked for an opinion by the Judge Advocate General. That opinion was such that he transmitted it to Attorney General A. Mitchell Palmer with a memorandum which said in part:

In the opinion of the Judge Advocate General the foregoing provisions as to the obligations upon the part of the Government are so wasteful and extravagant, and in view of the location of the plant in a foreign country, so inimical to the interests of the Government as to be beyond the power of any agent of the Government to incorporate them in a binding contract.

Mr. Palmer was not active in the quest of profiteers. He did nothing in this matter. On March 4, 1921, Mr. Weeks succeeded Mr. Baker and Mr. Daugherty succeeded Mr. Palmer. Mr. Weeks played out his predecessor's hand. He told the Assistant Secretary of War, Mr. Wainwright, to look into the matter. Mr. Wainwright did and again sent a copy of the papers in the case to the Department of Justice, with a strong note urging action in which this language appears:

I consider the terms of the contract as unconscionable and that suit should be instituted to recover from the company the sum of $1,750,000 loaned by the Government, plus unpaid interest from February 28, 1918.

But Mr. Daugherty was not active in the quest of profiteers, those days. Decidedly not. Mr. Lenihan and others in his department had those matters in hand; and Mr. Lenihan, according to the official statement of a member of his staff, had come to the conclusion that the prosecution "of war contractors generally" was "inadvisable" because it "would upset business conditions" and be "contrary to good policy." So no suit was brought.

Now then, for a third time, the evidence in this case has been collected and placed in the hands of the Attorney General with the request that court action be instituted to recover the money the War Department claims to be due from this contractor. Mr. Palmer is engaged in the private practice of law, and Mr. Lenihan's official duties in the Attorney General's office have taken him into fields not concerned with this piece of suggested litigation. The Weekly is informed that action will be forthcoming.

The evidence last submitted to the Department of Justice comes from the Air Service. It is the product of six months' careful investigation.

The American Electro Products Company was organized after our entry into the war by a group of Canadian and American capitalists who own the Shawinigan Water & Power Company and other enterprises of a similar character in the Province of Quebec. Among the holdings of the group was a concern which bears a name which is almost identical with that of the one we are writing about. It is called the Canadian Electro Products Company. It was organized to make glacial acetic acid for the British Government. Its plant is at Shawinigan Falls.

The processes by which this acid is made had been perfected by the Canadian concern, the machinery and the methods standardized. The same capitalists who controlled the Canadian works, with the same staffs of engineers and technical experts, undertaking to make the same sort of acid for the United States Government, therefore, were confronted by a simple problem. It was merely a matter of duplicating the Canadian plant; there were no risks or difficulties with such expensive experiments as added to the burdens of many war contractors embarking on new enterprises.

Early in 1918 representatives of the American Electro Products Company went to Washington—were summoned there, they say. There was much negotiation and at length, on February 28th, a contract was signed—forced upon them, say the A. E. P. representatives. Naturally, the A. E. P. being so reluctant in the matter, there were concessions, rather startling concessions. By the terms of the contract the United States made the A. E. P. a pres-

Photos © Harris & Ewing,
  from Paul Thompson

J. Mayhew Wain-
wright, Assistant
Secretary of War, who called the
terms of the Government's contract
with the American Electro Products
Company "unconscionable" and urged
institution of suit to recover $1,750,000

ent of a plant, estimated to cost $1,500,-
000, but which actually cost $1,750,000,
we paying for it just the same. When
the plant was built the A. E. P. was
to make 18,000 tons of acid at cost plus
9.442 cents a pound. Of this 9.442
cents, 1.112 cents was to be the company's profit and 8.33 cents was the
company's profit also, but was given
the name of "amortization," which
meant pay for the plant by the gradual
retirement of notes given by the company in return for funds advanced by
the United States to cover the cost of
erecting the plant.

The contract contained no cancellation clause except after the production
and sale of 9,000 tons of acid. The contract also stipulated that the A. E. P.
plant should be a complete industrial
unit, capable of independent operation.
This clause was inserted with a view
to government operation should the
builders default. It served another purpose in the end, and it may save American taxpayers about $4,200,000, or the
difference between $1,777,000, which the
War Department Claims Board felt the
Government should pay the A. E. P., and
about $2,500,000, which the Air Service
auditors claim the A. E. P. should pay
the Government.

The war ended before the plant was
completed, and shortly thereafter the
company filed a claim calling for:

(a) Cancellation of war credit
      notes $1,750,000
(b) Furnished by contractors to
      complete plant   402,000
(c) Paid by company to house
      laborers   100,000
(d) Profit on 9,000 tons of acid.   199,800
(e) Loss of coal   27,000

      Total.................... $2,478,800

The Claims Board induced
the claimant to eliminate all
but items (a) and (e), and on
March 4, 1920, Joseph Fair-
banks, then a vice-chairman of
the Claims Board, wrote that
the claim thus reduced to
$1,777,000 represented a settle-
ment that was "advantageous"
to the Government. He stated,
however, that he understood
an audit was being made and
that the settlement should be
subject to its findings.

A government auditor was
sent to Shawinigan Falls.
One of the first things he noted
was the scattered nature of
the buildings comprising the
A. E. P. plant. Inquiry re-
vealed that the most important
of them were not on the property
of the A. E. P. at all, but on land
owned by the sister corporation,
the Canadian Electro Products Company. While the A. E. P. produced
nothing, the buildings it erected with
American money on the C. E. P. property enabled the C. E. P. to double its
output of acid sold to the British Government. The auditor sent a map of
the property with his report, which
he says "indicates clearly that the company did not build or attempt to build
a modern and fully equipped plant'
in accordance with the provisions of the
contract. . . . But it appears that the
contractor purposely planned the con-
struction of the various units" so as to
make independent operation impossible.
The auditor declares the contractor
therefore defaulted in the performance
of his contract, and the Department of
Justice supports him in that view. Con-
tinuing, the auditor says in his report:

This contract is a most extraordinary
one. The company claimed that they were
summoned to Washington early in 1918 and
were requested to submit a proposition,
whereby they would manufacture the same
quality of acetic acid for the American
Government as was manufactured [by
them] for the British Government, and they further claimed
that they did not seek the contract and in fact did not want the
contract under any circumstances;
but finally in their effort to side-
step the matter they state that
they submitted figures and conditions which they felt fully confi-
dent would not be acceptable to
our Government, and admitting to
the writer that the terms were
unreasonable and very much out
of line. However, they further
stated that their proposal in general seemed very acceptable to
the officer in charge of the contract branch and the contract as
signed was executed purely on the
basis of this proposal.

The auditor indicates how
the Canadians put the bars up
higher and higher as the
negotiations pro-
ceeded. Several drafts
of the contract were
made before one was
sufficiently "unreason-
able" and "out of
line" to suit the A.
E. P. representatives.
Frank B. Maltby, a
New York engineer,
who surveyed the

plant, made a report which, to say the
least, shows no prejudice in favor of
the United States. He observes:

The contract is most extraordinary. . . .
The Government would pay the entire cost
of a plant costing more than $2,000,000
which was to become the company's property, pay the entire cost of manufacturing
the material contracted for plus a fixed
profit which would have amounted to $434,-
000. The total cost of the contract [to the
United States] would have been more than
$6,000,000.

It will be interesting to glance at a
few items in the cost of the plant, in-
dicating in what manner the A. E. P.
expended some of the money passed out
so liberally by the United States. Land
was bought for $37,632 or $2,000 an
acre. This land, according to unbiased
experts, was worth not to exceed $200
an acre, and furthermore it was bought
from the Shawinigan Water & Power
Company, owners of the A. E. P. Thus,
in effect, these capitalists reimbursed
themselves at the expense of the United
States for land they already owned,
paying ten times what that land was
worth. They reimbursed themselves
further to the extent of $12,144 for
clearing the land.

A carbide plant costing $396,968 and
a gas plant costing $34,291 were built
on the property of the Canadian Electro
Products Company with money the
United States supplied. The carbide
plant was used to make carbide to sell
to the British Government. It made
nothing for the United States. Forty-
five thousand dollars was spent on a
clubhouse for employees of both the
American and Canadian concerns, and
$9,745 went to fit up the basement of
one of the C. E. P. buildings as welfare
quarters. Five thousand five hundred
dollars of American money went to op-
erate the Cascade Inn, located in the
town of Shawinigan Falls and owned
by the Shawinigan Falls Water & Power
Company.

(Continued on page 28)

A. Mitchell Palmer,
former Attorney Gen-
eral, who received a
memorandum on the
A. E. P. case from
Newton D. Baker,
then Secretary of
War, but took no ac-
tion in the matter

That Man Hines
and His Job

An Interview With the New Head of the United States Veterans Bureau

General Frank T. Hines, photographed at his desk by a veteran taking vocational training

The ten-story Washington home of the Veterans Bureau—the capitol of American ex-servicedom

A VERY serene and undisturbed man sits at a large desk in a large room on the tenth floor of a building that takes up half of a block in Washington, D. C. The elevators have glass doors so that as you ascend you can see that the building is filled with people. A census would reveal a population of nearly 5,000. They all work for the man who has the big desk on the tenth floor, and who is the president of a great life and accident insurance company; the dean of schools in which there are 110,000 students learning everything from cobbling to civil engineering; the superintendent of a string of hospitals in which there are 26,000 patients, and the fiscal agent of the Federal Government in transactions which involve the outlay of several million dollars a week. The 5,000 in Washington comprise only a small part of the forces required to conduct the diverse enterprises entrusted to the man at the big desk. Twenty-five thousand others are on the pay-rolls for which he is responsible.

The organization thus briefly described is the United States Veterans Bureau. The man at the desk is the director. His name is Frank T. Hines.

One of the most dependable of Washington newspapermen, an experienced correspondent who has watched men of affairs come and go for twenty years, has sized Hines up in about these words:

"He is another Charles G. Dawes, minus the Hell-and-Maria stuff. He has all of Dawes's administrative skill and force without the latter's explosiveness."

It is a pretty apt contrast. Dawes is a musician, Hines a mathematician. I have been told it is mental recreation for him to sit down and work out a problem in trigonometry. Now trigonometry is simple; nothing is simpler or more fascinating to the man who knows it and has a bent for that sort of thing. There is a right solution for everything, and you can't miss it if your procedure is correct. Geometry is considered easier than trig, and Hines describes

the Veterans Bureau job as a problem in plane geometry; namely, to find the shortest distance between two points—a problem in administrative geometry, as it were.

He goes at his work with the precision, the ease and the confidence of a mathematical expert. No Hell-and-Maria stuff, no desk pounding for him. Whoever heard of a mathematical problem being solved by those means? Now one is apt to associate the mathematical mind with a quality of austere coldness, which would be to reckon amiss in the case of Hines. Rather short of stature and slight of build—a bit lean and wiry—the restful countenance of a scholar; kindly eyes; a soft, pleasant voice; a most engaging smile which shows itself just ever so often—such is Hines, a student of the most inexorable of the sciences, it is true, but a most understanding and sympathetic student, also, of the most variable of them, to wit, the science of human nature. It is a rare combination, and one hard to beat.

Hines works hard. He is at his desk at half-past eight in the morning and usually he is there until ten or eleven at night. But he has forty-five minutes for lunch and an hour and a half for dinner. They are periods of real recreation. He never carries his office problems beyond his office door, and thus begins each day refreshed. He is thriving, physically, on a job that has made bodily wrecks of all of his predecessors. It is the power of detachment and concentration that enables him to do it.

He is one of your impersonal leaders, a type too rarely found in public life, a type common to great undertakings of business. In the big scheme that is being worked out in the mammoth Veterans Bureau the quiet Hines seems merely to fit in, but actually he directs and dominates.

A moment before the conversation which is about to be related took place Director Hines was making arrangements to procure the 300,000 tons of coal his hospitals will require next winter. A little while before that he was talking to a student in one of his schools. This young veteran is taking vocal lessons. The school wants to jump the tuition from $4 to $7 for half an hour's instruction, which seemed a little stiff, but the director wanted the student's thought in the matter. The same forenoon there had been a conference with investigators who are gathering data for the committee of the United States Senate which is preparing to launch its inquiry into the charges of waste and poor management in the conduct of the bureau's affairs before General Hines came in.

On top of all this a reporter for the Weekly called to ask the general what he thought of his new job, which has been called the most difficult post the Government has to offer. When General Hines took it on March 1st one candid friend said he wanted to extend his sympathy rather than his congratu-

lations. General Hines smiled when the reporter mentioned the incident. "My problem is really quite simple," he began in a pleasant voice. There was assurance in his tone, but no cocksureness. He did not pound his desk as he spoke. Hines is not a desk-pounder. He picked up a pencil.

"We have the man who needs relief," continued Director Hines, drawing a small circle on a piece of paper. "We have the relief." He drew another circle. "Our problem is to unite the two. That can be done by constructing, in terms of organization and administration, the most direct line of communication connecting the man in need and the thing he is in need of." The director used his pencil again, and here is a faithful reproduction of the diagram he had completed:

O————————O

"Now then," he went on, "though simple, the job is not quite so simple

as my illustration might imply. We are not starting with a clean sheet." He crumpled the diagram he had made and took a fresh piece of paper. "We have not only the man, here, and the relief, over here, but also we have a road connecting the two. But the road is not a straight road, such as would lend the best facilities to traffic. It runs this way." The director employed his pencil again, putting the finishing touches to a sketch that resembled this:

"Now, if I can cut out some of these byways and detours and reduce this long and circuitous road to a short and direct one I will have succeeded in my job; I will have performed the task the President asked me to come here and take in hand. This will not be done too quickly. I would be very foolhardy
(Continued on page 16)

How *to* Get *a* Job *in* Paris (Ha! Ha!)

By Bernhard Ragner

FROM: Buddy in Paris.
TO: Buddy Back Home Hankering for Gay Paree.
SUBJECT: Jobs in Paris.

1. You have written asking if it is a safe proposition to come to Paris, without any promise of work, armed only with good intentions and a few hundred francs, Yes, it is perfectly safe—
IF you have discovered the secret of living without eating; or
IF you are so constituted that you can subsist on a diet of beautiful vistas and French sunsets.
But unless you can, you had better stick to the home sector, for being jobless and francless in Paris is as safe as playing with matches in a gunpowder factory.

2. You also ask for the naked truth about the job situation in Paris. I will give it frankly. You won't believe it, but here it is: Rotten, rottener, rottenest. That's the straight dope, in all its ugliness, without varnish or talcum powder. Of course, if you are crazy enough to come to Paris minus funds and minus a job, this confidential tip won't deter you one bit.

3. Your homesickness for Paris is possibly so acute that nothing can prevent you from taking the perilous step. But I warn you in advance that starving to death in Paris is as painful and prosaic as starving to death anywhere else, while cabling home for funds is not the most pleasurable or dignified sensation in the world. And you surely don't want to come home in the "bum boat," as some five hundred of your buddies did a few months ago.

4. To get one of the few jobs that do exist for Americans in Paris requires a miraculous combination of get-up, good luck and genius. Why? Because there is a famine of jobs and a surplus of job-hunters. "Barkis is willin'," more than willing, but Paris is crowded with Barkises. Everybody's doing it, for job-hunting is one of the principal pastimes of Americans in France (ex-

cepting the tourists), and when an American really gets a job he hangs on to it as a miser sticks to his gold. Worst of all for the newcomer, few of the job-holders die and none resign. When a vacancy does occur, the boss generally has a friend, and the unknown job-chaser is left out in the cold, cold rain—it still falls occasionally.

5. In the months following the departure of the A. E. F. getting a job was comparable to rolling off a log if you had any services worth selling. Most of the welfare agencies kept on operating. The American Graves Registration Service gave employment to hundreds. France enjoyed a post-war business boom, and jobs for Americans could really be found. Them days is gone forever. The welfare agencies have parte'ed, except two or three whose personnel is chiefly French. (French labor, manual or mental, is cheaper, you know.) The A. G. R. S. has completed its task and its employees have been scattered. French commerce has suffered severe reverses, and finding a job with a French firm (for an American) is like getting a war profiteer into heaven.

6. So what is left? Well, there is always the embassy; then the consulate general. But here nobody dies and nobody resigns. Even if they did, unless you are a friend of Congressman Andy Gump your name is mud. Then come the American banks, newspapers, and tourist agencies, but here specialized knowledge and experience are required, plus being on hand exactly the second that a vacancy occurs. Generally the man on the job hangs on to the bitter end, although once in a while there is an opening. (The century plant is also noted for blooming at certain intervals.) As for most of the American firms with Paris offices, they are glad just now if they can pay their telephone bills, for the exchange fluctuations have knocked them into a cocked hat, or something worse. Decreased profits mean fewer employees, and only the ghost of a chance for you, my boy!

7. You have a colossal nerve, anyhow, in imagining that you could get a job with your invisible, inaudible, incomprehensible French. Ah oui, you can say "comme ça," "très bien," and "combien." But that's only a flea-bite in the ocean. To land a job and hold it, in Paris, you must parler français like a mademoiselle. Even with American firms a fluent mastery of French is required, since most of your deals are with Frenchmen who positively do not comprehend the doughboy dialect of their language.

8. But, you say, there must be some jobs somewhere in France. Most certainly, but you wouldn't take them. If you want to pilot a pick or be chauffeur to a shovel, earn 500 or 600 francs a month, the pleasure is all yours. Foreign labor is being used quite extensively in the devastated regions, and a few Americans, swallowing their pride, have taken jobs as manual laborers merely to prevent the Death Angel from paying a visit. I know one man who speaks four languages but who digs ditches at 700 francs a month because he can't get anything else. He does this for the sake of his French wife and baby.

9. Let the fatal fact be admitted: Paris is a paradise for the plutocrat, but hell for the poverty stricken. I know you don't belong to the latter class yet, but if you come to Paris, unless you have beaucoup dollars you soon will. For the francs disappear as speedily as A.W.O.L.'s before an M.P. And the Champs Elysées, while lovely to gaze upon, cannot be eaten.

Here is my parting, paternal advice: Whether you can safely undertake the Paris adventure depends entirely upon the state of your exchequer. If it bulges with one-hundred dollar bills you are perfectly safe in coming to Paris, but to do so with a limited number of francs is to invite disaster and defy common sense. It is as dangerous as going over the top—and remember this: There's no glory in being knocked off in the Battle of Paris in 1923.

To Batch or Not to Batch

By Atwood H. Townsend

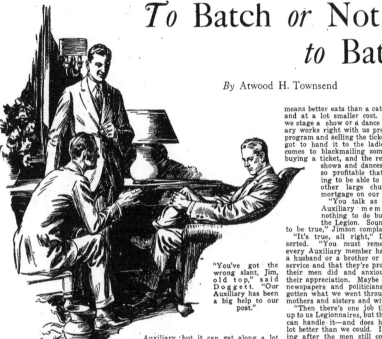

"You've got the wrong slant, Jim, old top," said Doggett. "Our Auxiliary has been a big help to our post."

"**Y**ES, sir," declared Doggett, "I've been married a long time now — nearly eight months—and I haven't a kick coming yet."

"Marvelous!" said Jimson.

"Stupendous!" I exclaimed.

The three of us, buddies in the same outfit overseas, had met at the department convention of the Legion, and now that the official doings had finished we were holding our own private convention.

"You can batch it as long as you want to," the new benedict insisted, "but sooner or later some woman will capture you and make you like it. And the reason is that, although you can get along fairly well without a wife, you can get along a lot better with one."

"The deuce you can!" objected Jimson, who was a hard-boiled woman-hater.

I didn't say anything, because to tell the truth I was thinking of a certain girl who—but that's another story.

"We could have fought the war without the help of any women, some folks will tell you," Doggett went on, "but you've got to admit that the ladies of the Red Cross and the Salvation Army and the Y.M.C.A. did a good deal to keep the old morale at a hundred per cent efficiency. Same way a Legion post can get along fairly well without an Auxiliary, but it can get along a lot better with one."

"Whoa, there, brother," put in Jimson. "I disagree with you on that point. Our post hasn't any Auxiliary and doesn't want to have one, thank the Lord. Why should a gang of ex-soldiers have to be pestered by a bunch of women holding tea parties and tying pink ribbons all around the Legion clubrooms?"

"You've got the wrong slant, Jim, old top," said Doggett. "Our Auxiliary has been a big help to our post. If you belong to a bachelor post, then all I can say is that your outfit isn't doing its full job, is missing half its opportunities."

I sat back, keeping my ears trained on the argument that followed, for my own post was thinking about stirring up an Auxiliary for itself and I wanted to collect all the dope I could on the question.

"Honestly, now," the skeptical Jimson queried, "isn't your Auxiliary more bother than it's worth?"

"Not by a long shot. On the contrary, the women have done a lot more for us than we have for them. And I think you'll find the same thing true of almost every Auxiliary unit in the country. You must remember that the first objective of the Auxiliary is to help The American Legion and its members, and, judging from what I've seen myself, I've got to testify that the Auxiliary makes good. Take our outfit, for instance. When the post puts on a dinner the Auxiliary takes care of cooking and serving it, and that means better eats than a caterer's feed, and at a lot smaller cost. Whenever we stage a show or a dance the Auxiliary works right with us preparing the program and selling the tickets. You've got to hand it to the ladies when it comes to blackmailing somebody into buying a ticket, and the result is our shows and dances have been so profitable that we're going to be able to pay off another large chunk of the mortgage on our clubhouse."

"You talk as though the Auxiliary members had nothing to do but work for the Legion. Sounds too good to be true," Jimson complained.

"It's true, all right," Doggett asserted. "You must remember that every Auxiliary member had a son or a husband or a brother or a father in the service and that they're proud of what their men did and anxious to show their appreciation. Maybe some of the newspapers and politicians have forgotten what we went through, but our mothers and sisters and wives haven't.

"Then there's one job that's really up to us Legionnaires, but the Auxiliary can handle it—and does handle it—a lot better than we could. I mean looking after the men still cooped up in hospitals. Believe me, that's where the Auxiliary gets in some of its best work. Another thing that our Auxiliary has done is the giving of unobtrusive and practical help to the families of local ex-service men who were down on their luck—clothes for the youngsters, help in getting employment, even loans to tide them over temporary difficulties. Oh, there are plenty of ways our Auxiliary has helped our post. About all we've ever done in return has been to give a party in their honor.

"Take my word for it, the bachelor posts are missing something. There have even been some interesting by-products. For instance, there was a man in our post who was a good sort of a skate but afraid of the women, something like Jimson here."

"I'm not afraid of them," Jimson protested. "I just prefer to get along without them."

"As I was saying when interrupted with such atrocious rudeness," Doggett gazed sternly at Jimson, "this bashful Legionnaire happened to meet at one of our joint parties an Auxiliary member, sister of one of the boys, who didn't scare him a bit. Now they have a candidate for the S. O. L., the Sons of Legionnaires. So you see that all kinds of benefits are apt to result from establishing an Auxiliary unit in connection with a Legion post."

"The Auxiliary has certainly justified its existence in the case of your post," I agreed.

"Yes, but one swallow doesn't make

(Continued on page 25)

From Your Post, Your Unit, Your Townsfolk, Yourself

WANTED: $100,000 *by* May 30

WHERE THE GRAVES FUND STANDS

To March 31st .	$9,492.45
Week ending April 6th . .	1,635.51
Total to April 6th	$11,127.96

THE American Legion Overseas Graves Endowment Fund is becoming an issue with America's veterans. Legion posts throughout the country are making the issue. The raising of at least $100,000 is no slight affair, even for an organization of eleven thousand units, and the units know it.

In its last issue the Weekly called attention to the accomplishment of Carl A. Johnson Post of Grand Rapids, Michigan, in raising more than $1,200 with the co-operation of the Grand Rapids *Herald.* Succeeding mails indicated that other posts were undertaking identical campaigns. No other post got quite the start made by Johnson Post, however and therein lies one of the difficulties of the work. On Memorial Day every cent of the $100,000 should be raised, with a neat surplus left over, and little time is left before Memorial Day. For that reason posts everywhere are urged not to delay their campaigns; too much money *cannot* be raised to insure proper decoration of the 32,000 overseas graves.

So it is that announcements of contributions so far have to do largely with the gifts of individuals—the spontaneous offerings of men and women who read the Weekly and who feel a sense of individual obligation above the obligation of their posts and Auxiliary units.

Such men, for example, are seven disabled ex-service men and women in a North Dakota tuberculosis sanitorium at Dunseith. March was a month of blizzards and deep snows where they were located and Memorial Day must have seemed far away to them, yet they got together their dollars for an early contribution to the fund.

It was a March of sunshine in California when another disabled man, living in a National Soldiers Home, pinned a bill to a letter in which he said. "I never like to owe anybody anything if I can help it, and I feel as though this is a dollar I do owe to the Graves Endowment Fund."

Across the continent George J. Merambellioutakis on that same day was posting from the Connecticut State Hospital at Middletown a letter containing his own contribution in memory of the comrades he had known who now lie in France and Belgium.

On that day also, Miss Marion L. Humphrey, a nurse in United States Veterans' Hospital No. 76 at Maywood, Illinois, sent forward a post office money order as her tribute to the men whom she had helped in life. She remembered the days when flag-covered stretchers were being carried out from the wards of suffering in France and taps was sounding from the cemeteries.

On another day of the same week two former chaplains sent contributions from widely separated sections. From the Catholic University of America in Washington, D. C., the Rev. Fr. Michael

THE American Legion Graves Endowment Fund will be invested in perpetuity and the income used annually to provide decorations for the graves of 32,000 American soldiers and sailors whose bodies will forever lie in American cemeteries overseas. At least $100,000 is needed to increase the principal of this fund, which has as its nucleus a million francs now on deposit in France.

The Weekly publishes in every issue a list of contributors who have given one dollar or more to the Graves Endowment Fund. Owing to the necessity for re-checking this list to insure accuracy and prevent omissions, it is a few days behind the total as given in the figures above. Names of contributing Legion posts and Auxiliary units are printed in boldface type.

Checks for the Graves Endowment Fund should be made payable to the National Treasurer, The American Legion, and addressed to him at National Headquarters, The American Legion, Indianapolis, Ind.

CONTRIBUTIONS

The following contributions are acknowledged:

ARIZONA. *Phoenix:* Austin I. Grimes, $1.
ARKANSAS. *Ft. Smith:* G. M. Burrow, $2.
CALIFORNIA. *Beaumont:* **Summit Post, $5;** *Hemet:* **H. W. Hyland Post, $10;** *Madera:* **Madera Post, $5;** *Niles:* **Washington Township Post, $5;** *Soldiers Home:* Frederick Gibson, $1.
CONNECTICUT. *Ansonia:* G. J. Merambellioutakis, $5.
DISTRICT OF COLUMBIA. *Washington:* Mary C. Kell, $1; Rev. M. J. McKeough, $1.
FLORIDA. *Marianna:* Jas. W. Cullens, $1.50.
GEORGIA. *Atlanta:* W. W. Steed, $1.
ILLINOIS. *Avon:* Elmina Shinkel, $2.50; *Chi-*
(Continued on page 22)

J. McKeough, expressed his heartiest sympathy for the fund. He is chaplain of William Heesacker Post of De Pere, Wisconsin. From Wanatah, Ind., the Rev. D. L. Faurote sent his "chaplain's mite" and wished "success to the holy cause."

From every part of the country have come similar expressions of deep feeling by men and women who know best the sacrifices of those who died.

In proportion to numbers of members, The American Legion Auxiliary is bidding fair to surpass the Legion itself. In a single mail contributions were received from Auxiliary units in Fairhaven, Massachusetts; Lancaster, Pennsylvania; Windom, Minnesota; Oklahoma City, Oklahoma; Alpena, Michigan, and Indianapolis, Indiana.

Many of the Legion posts sending contributions announced they had not completed raising funds locally and would send additional amounts later. Many of the individual contributors said their posts would also send in contributions and pledged their help in raising the additional funds.

Charles A. Learned Post of Detroit submitted the first list of contributions which it has received since announcing the fund to its members and stated it would send in additional contributions at the end of each week. It announced it would receive public contributions through a Detroit newspaper during one week in April, following the plan of Johnson Post of Grand Rapids. Other posts in all parts of the country have adopted the plan of enlisting their communities in this national effort, and newspapers invariably are welcoming the opportunity of assisting by acknowledging the contributions made.

The Legion department of Mississippi has forwarded a list of the first thirty-eight contributions made through its department headquarters. The plan of forwarding contributions as received is favored by the National Treasurer. National Executive Committeemen of all States have been asked by National Commander Alvin Owsley to help obtain early action on the endowment fund by posts, and they are working with other department officials for this purpose. Department commanders and adjutants have forwarded personal appeals to posts explaining the importance of making this effort to insure perpetual decoration of the graves overseas represent the unanimous will of the Legion.

Legion officials who are watching the growth of the fund are highly gratified at the increase in the number of contributing posts and Auxiliary units shown in the list of contributors published this week. No less than 31 posts and units (including one notable contribution of $100 from Chicago 40 and 8-ers) are represented in this week's list, as against only 16 last week. Many individual contributions, of course, have been sent through posts.

THERE is, or was some time ago, a sign posted in the town of Livingston, California, which in speaking for a single community manages to express the feelings of virtually the entire Pacific Coast. This sign reads:

NO JAPANESE WANTED HERE

In a previous article, based like the present one on the report of the National Oriental Committee of The American Legion, I attempted to sum up the case of the Pacific Coast against the Japanese by saying that certain racial characteristics of the latter made it impossible for them to live amicably with their white neighbors. That is true enough, but it does not entirely account for that blunt sign in Livingston; incompatibility of temperament may be ground for divorce, but there is no reason why the separated pair cannot continue to live in the same town. Yet what that sign means exactly, with the approval of a large section of the Pacific Coast, is a separation measured in terms of miles; the Japanese are not wanted in the town, in the State or in the country.

It so happens that the explanation of this extreme position is right now one of the issues in the general discussion of immigration; it has to do with the attitude of the immigrant, any immigrant, toward his adopted land. We do not ask of him that he put on an American point of view as quickly and as easily as he puts on a ready-made suit of American clothes. We do not expect him to forget his native land, any more than we expect the man in Chicago to forget his Texas homestead. What we do expect — and demand — is that he shall not at any time regard the United States merely as a province of the mother country. If that is his attitude we don't want him, and that is why the Pacific Coast doesn't want Japanese.

There are many Japanese associations in the United States, more particularly in the West. The larger ones, such as the United North American Japanese Association, hold jurisdiction over an extended territory, sometimes covering several States. Under each of these larger organizations are local associations. All of them, in turn, are subject in large degree to the orders of the resident Japanese consul. By means of this interlocking control and supervision a high degree of discipline is maintained among the Japanese. These organizations constitute, in fact,

© *International*

Japanese school at Penryn, California

The Facts of the Japanese Question

Part II of a Summary of the Report of the Legion's National Oriental Committee

By Parkhurst Whitney

Buddhist temple in a California town.

an inner government by means of which the rule of the Japanese government is made effective over all members of the race living in this country.

You think that is moonshine? Then let the National Oriental Committee step aside for a moment and give the floor to Dr. Yoshi Saburo Kuno, professor at the University of California and son of General Kuno of the Japanese Army. He says:

The Japanese are not living in this state

(California) as emigrants. In my opinion they are establishing plantations of their own, introducing their peculiar civilization and governmental as well as educational institutions right in the midst of American civilization. With the recognition of their home government through their consulate offices they have established a sort of quasi-government in leading cities, towns and districts, wherever the size of the Japanese population warrants. They levy a tax on Japanese males and Japanese families under the caption of a membership tax.

In the state of California, the Japanese government maintains two consulate officers; viz., a consulate general at San Francisco and a consulate at Los Angeles. Under the control of each of these offices there is one central Japanese association. Under the control of each central association there are in turn numerous local Japanese associations. For example, the Central Japanese Association of San Francisco has forty local associations under its control, while the one at Los Angeles has twelve.

In case a local association should disobey, conduct itself with too great independence, or commit any irregularity, the consul general's office, upon the advice of the central association, would deprive it of all rights and privileges, such as the issuing of certificates.

The Japanese in the State hold an annual assembly corresponding somewhat to the California State Assembly. This assembly is composed of delegates sent by the local associations. There is also another assembly held annually which may be likened to the California State Senate in that only the managers of the various local associations are entitled to sit in that august body.

The purpose of the Japanese associations, quoting from the regulations of that in Berkeley, is "to defend, protect and guard Japanese interests and privileges against the outside, and to maintain and establish unity and harmony in the inside that they may enjoy full benefits."

This system of government within a government is strengthened by other practices, all of which illustrate the way in which the Japanese look upon that section of the United States which lies along the Pacific Ocean. The Japanese government permits its subjects, whether born at home or in a foreign country, to swear off allegiance to the mother country by signing a form called "Declaration of Losing Nationality," and this must be done before the child, if a male, reaches seventeen years of age, otherwise he must first complete (*Continued on page 22*)

EDITORIAL

For God and Country, we associate ourselves together for the following purposes: To uphold and defend the Constitution of the United States of America; to maintain law and order; to foster and perpetuate a one hundred percent Americanism; to preserve the memories and incidents of our association in the Great War; to inculcate a sense of individual obligation to the community, state and nation; to combat the autocracy of both the classes and the masses; to make right the master of might; to promote peace and good will on earth; to safeguard and transmit to posterity the principles of justice, freedom and democracy; to consecrate and sanctify our comradeship by our devotion to mutual helpfulness.—Preamble to Constitution of The American Legion.

Why There Must Be a Legion

MOST men see only those things that are near at hand. The farmer notes the sprouting wheat of his field rather than the trees of the forest. The ditch-digger concerns himself with good red clay and not with blue sky.

The average Legionnaire probably gives little thought to the policies of the national organization. He is proud of its achievements, but the thing that bothers him is whether the post dance will be a success, whether the next meeting will be lively enough to warrant giving up a date to go to the movies.

Comradeship is the Legion's reason for being; the keeping alive of the memories of the Great War. This it is that strikes home to every man.

Would the memories, the comradeship, live anyway?

Recently two buddies met again for the first time since the whizz-bang days near Montfaucon. They had been fox-hole mates then. They had vowed, each to himself after the manner of Anglo-Saxons, that such a friendship, born amid danger and thriving on mutual esteem, must never perish. They talked of the reunions when they got back. Nothing must interfere, even though one infantryman lived in Texas and the other in Illinois, and one was affluent and the other poor.

Their chance meeting the other day was marked by constraint. They found they had been living in the same town for a year and only a few blocks from each other. Each explained lamely why he hadn't written. Each pleaded the press of peace-time pursuits. "You know how it is—"

They realized they were traveling different paths, had different circles of acquaintance, different ambitions. They had been blood-brothers once. Now they were strangers.

Comradeship is perishable, sad as that may be. Men must have common interests to maintain friendship. Granted that such holy comradeship as that of the late war deserves to survive, men must ally themselves in an organization, some organization, that brings them together and keeps them interested in each other. They must again accomplish, and not content themselves with re-living the past. They must advance, not stand still. To keep old days alive there must be an American Legion.

Dalzell, J. M., Pvt., A. B.

PRIVATE DALZELL, most widely known of Civil War veterans who served in the ranks, is to receive his degree of bachelor of arts from Washington and Jefferson College at this June's commencement. Sixty-three years ago he was a presumably innocent freshman, but barely had the class of 1864, of which he was a member, got by heart the college yell than they had to substitute for it the battle cry. Into the war plunged Student Dalzell, to remain a private in spite of commissions that were actually tendered him. Less than ten years after the war he organized a grand reunion of privates, though he invited "the generals, too, if they can behave themselves and keep quiet." William Tecumseh Sherman, apparently convinced of his own capacities for decorum and taciturnity, came and presided.

In this issue of the Weekly is told the story of another soldier, now director of the United States Veterans' Bureau, who left college to go to the wars twenty-five years ago and who has only recently received the degree which he would have earned in course if the sabres had not started rattling. Better late than never. But Frank T. Hines is now a general. Cannot a grateful Government at last bestow upon J. M. Dalzell his corporal's warrant?

Fresh, Gay War

GLORIFICATION of war is as much out of fashion as the Kaiser's mustachios. In the days when swinishness was a cult in pre-war Prussia and swashbucklers like Von Bernhardi regarded insulting arrogance as a superior and strictly military virtue, militarists of the old school longed for a first-class war in order that the German youth might be duly ennobled. They longed for war—"fresh, gay war"—much as one might wish for a thunderstorm on a muggy day—it would make everybody feel better.

Events the world over during the last five years have shown the sophistry of the doctrine of national purification by strife. And we doubt if there is lingering at this late day in any country the illusion that its wartime Army was composed exclusively of shining knights, crusaders, heroes and martyrs. On the contrary, it is admitted that war has not changed human nature much. The individual has tended to emerge from it with much the same qualities, virtues and vices, that he had when he went into it—and the tendency is true alike of civilians and fighting men.

The former premier of Italy, Francisco Nitti, in his recent book, "The Wreck of Europe," blames war's reaction on unchanged human nature for the unrest and trouble he sees in his own country and her neighbors. He writes:

What is most urgently required at the moment is to change the prevalent war mentality which still infects us and overcomes all generous sentiments, all hopes of unity. The statement that war makes men better or worse is, perhaps, an exaggerated one. War, which creates a state of exaltation, hypertrophies all the qualities, all the tendencies, be they for good or for evil. Ascetic souls, spirits naturally noble, being disposed toward sacrifice, develop a state of exaltation and true fervor. How many examples of nobility, of abnegation, of voluntary martyrdom has not the war given us. But in persons disposed to evil actions, in rude and violent spirits (and these are always in the majority), the spirit of violence increases. This spirit, which, among the intellectuals takes the form of arrogance and concupiscence, and in politics expresses itself in a policy of conquest, assumes in the crowd the most violent forms of class war, continuous assaults upon the power of the state, and an unbalanced desire to gain as much as possible with the least possible work. Before the war the number of men ready to take the law into their own hands was relatively small; now there are many such individuals.

If we accept the principle that men get out of war only an intensification of the qualities they put into it, it is comforting to recall such manifestations of The American Legion's after-the-war spirit as National Education Week, the national essay contest and the national employment campaign.

A Fable

ONCE upon a time two nations engaged in a great war, and in the course of time the entire world became involved. After many years of ruthless warfare the weaker nations at last met defeat. A truce was called and the diplomats of the victorious nations met to discuss the terms of a peace treaty.

These diplomats sought to establish a precedent and repaired to the battlefields to hold their conference. They carried all their luggage and slept in pup tents. Three times each day they fell into line and were served the rations of the soldier in the field.

The conference lasted less than forty-eight hours. A peace treaty was drawn up and accepted by all the nations, and the entire world lived in peace for a long time after.

Ah Sing Ching, the thirteen-year-oldster who won the 1922 National American Legion Essay Contest, feeds his father's chickens just outside the main entrance of the Ching family home in Hawaii

By

Andrew Farrell

Ah Sing Ching—American

AH SING CHING, winner of first prize in The American Legion's national essay contest, is a resident of Honouliuli, District of Ewa, Island of Oahu, Territory of Hawaii. He is a potential American citizen of Chinese descent (which is not at all the same thing as being Chinese), and was born at Honouliuli May 14, 1909. He has an intelligent, good-humored face surmounted by stiff and unruly black hair; and, as he can go barefooted all the year, he can wriggle his toes remarkably. He will finish at Ewa school this summer; thence he will go to McKinley High in Honolulu; from McKinley to the University of Hawaii for two years, and then to Cornell, which he has heard highly commended, for two years more. By that time he will have learned much chemistry, so he will return to Ewa plantation and ask "Young" George Renton, the manager, for a job.

It was last summer that Ah Sing first desired to emulate the chemists of Ewa sugar mill. A brother, now in McKinley High, having a like ambition had fired the lad. "But will you change your mind?" Ah Sing was asked. His sister Florence replied for him. "I think," said the little lady, "that it is much better for him to be on a plantation than in an office. It is better for his health. And if he changes his mind I'll spank him."

That breath-consuming amount of data is well out of the way, for now the story may be told of how Mrs. Katherine Burke, principal of Ah Sing's school, took the good news of the lad's success in the essay contest to Honouliuli. Mr. Renton had a telephone call from Honolulu. He immediately wrote a note to Mrs. Burke. Grasping the paper, she summoned a Japanese taxi man and hastened to the Chings' home.

Florence received the note from Mrs. Burke, who may have been a trifle too excited to speak. Florence read what Mr. Renton had written, that Ah Sing had won $750. She smiled, laughed, and hard on the heels of the laugh began to weep. Came her mother, Wong Keau, to hear the news in shrill little English. Followed Ah Sing. Gratified and perhaps surprised—despite his reiterated predictions that he would win, he heard and laughed and disappeared. It is possible that he also wept.

Wong Keau and Florence seated themselves and rocked to and fro and laughed and cried. The sympathetic Japanese driver emulated them: "Gee, too bad! Gee, too bad!" And from the mother, in praise of the teachers who had made her son's victory possible by explaining to him The American Legion's aims: "Too much hard work teachers do with my boys. Too much

The prize essayist in the bosom of his family. Left to right, Florence, sister; Wong Keau, mother; Tai Shia Gsu, consul for China; Ah Sing himself; a brother, graduate of the McKinley High School in Honolulu; a brother, now attending the McKinley High School

good to my children. Plenty good teachers my boys have." After a time, when Mrs. Burke was returning to Ewa, this from the bewildered Japanese: "Wha's the matter? Plenty *pilikia* (trouble)! No *pilikia!* Plenty *pilikia!* No *pilikia!*" And indeed the to-do of the women must have disconcerted the son of Nippon.

This bit of drama occurred at the dwelling of the Chings, a roughly-built house off the Ewa-Waipahu road. The hypercritical might describe the structure as a shack, but it is whitewashed within and is as neat as the proverbial pin. So is the yard, which, after the Oriental fashion, has not one blade of grass to mar the monotony of bare earth. From near at hand come the cackle of chickens and the hiss of geese. In the mid-distance is the tender green of young rice sprouting in paddy fields; beyond, the blue water of Pearl Harbor and three wireless towers of the naval station; and above the eastern horizon peers Diamond Head. It overlooks Honolulu, whither Ah Sing had journeyed twice in thirteen years before different clubs began to make a luncheon orator of him. ("Were you nervous?" Ah Sing was asked. "No," he replied in clipped English. "I have spoken in school.")

The Chings did not always live in the house just described. Once they occupied another nearby. In the two dwellings were born fourteen children, and one saw light in China. Four are

dead, and there remain eleven. Four are girls and seven (with an apologetic bow to Florence) are of that so-eminently desirable and heaven-blessed male sex.

It was twenty-five years ago that the Chings departed from South China for Hawaii. The family prospered, as Chinese are prone to do. Ching Sen, the father, is part owner of a pork and provision shop in Waipahu. He speaks some English.

Stout is Wong Keau, the mother, and still young (how she would click her tongue deprecatingly at that!), with a merry face that smiles readily, and cheeks rosy under the yellow pigment of her skin. Picture her, laden with firecrackers and other supplies for the Chinese New Year, descending from an automobile and insisting that her visitors return to the house. In the dwelling more speech, carried on in pidgin English interlarded with Hawaiian. "This *makule*," explains Wong Keau with the grace of a duchess. Her deprecating hand encompasses the house that she admits is "old"; but, she continues smilingly, "too poor, too poor." An uncomprehending Caucasian might stare at her jewelry; but jade and gold, Wong Keau, are they not very dear to the heart of a Chinese woman? And how can you describe yourself as "too poor" when you have eleven children, of whom the half-grinning Ah Sing and the eager-eyed Florence are two?

But eager and intelligent though

Florence may be, she cannot quite explain who are the Chinese gentlemen pictured in a print on the wall. Persons of consequence, evidently, for "punk sticks" have been burning before them. In the yard, too, stands a little green shrine, empty except for a wee china bowl and a receptacle for more sticks. Gods without; gods within; "something," Florence hazards, "like Japanese Buddha." To press Ah Sing for information is useless. "I don't know anything about this religion," says he with a trace of—call it impatience. "Then what is yours?" He is puzzled. "You haven't chosen any yet?" "No."

Knows little of "this religion," does Ah Sing, and he speaks Cantonese poorly. Like many Chinese, he turns from the path of his ancestors, and his parents, with little show of emotion, watch him depart. Sons of a sturdy race, he and his brothers and Japanese cousins have almost completely supplanted the Hawaiians in the land. "When we come here," says Wong Keau, "ten houses of natives. Now all *make* (dead)."

But the Chinese and Japanese will not be all *make*. They will remain, they and their remote descendants, all native-born American citizens. To Americanize them is a tremendous task. But not a hopeless one—not when Ah Sing of Honouliuli can win in a national contest with the Marys and Williams of the States.

No Back Pay for Air Service Cadets

AN adverse decision has just been handed down by the United States Supreme Court in the case of Nelson W. Rider vs. the United States, which has been pending on appeal for the past year. The Court of Claims, before which the case was first tried, ruled that former Air Service Cadets, who originally had received special pay of $100 a month and had been later reduced to $33 a month, the pay of a first-class private, were entitled to collect back pay to bring their total pay

up to $100 for the period spent in training. In addition, it was held, they were entitled to flight pay of fifty percent of the regular pay.

The decision of the Court of Claims was immediately appealed to the United States Supreme Court, as the Rider case was a test case, approximately ten thousand former Air Service Cadets have been closely watching the outcome. Chief Justice Taft, in delivering the opinion of the Supreme Court, held that the act of June 15, 1917, intended

that the cadets should receive $100 a month only up to June 30, 1918, the end of the fiscal year. Its enactment, the Court held, was "to put enlisted men on a level with civilians going through the same training for commissions in the Reserve Corps." It was a "temporary leveling up," and denied the $100 a month pay after June 30, after which date no provision was made to pay civilians in training for commissions. The Supreme Court decision definitely closes this matter.

Little Known Facts of History   *By* Wallgren

KING TUTANKAMEN NEVER USED A TYPEWRITER

JULIUS CAESAR NEVER WORE SUSPENDERS

WISE KING SOLOMON NEVER USED A TELEPHONE

METHUSELAH NEVER SMOKED A PIPE

QUEEN ELIZABETH NEVER DANCED THE "SHIMMIE"

KING RICHARD III NEVER RODE IN A FLIVVER

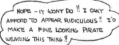

SIR WALTER RALEIGH NEVER WORE A FOUR-IN-HAND NECKTIE

KING HENRY VIII NEVER USED A SAFETY RAZOR

CHRISTOPHER COLUMBUS NEVER CHEWED TOBACCO

CAPT. KIDD NEVER WORE A DERBY HAT

ALEXANDER THE GREAT NEVER WORE A HIGH STARCHED COLLAR

GENERAL PERSHING NEVER SHOT CRAPS WITH THE ENLISTED MEN IN THE A.E.F.

You, US & Co. 1923

That Man Hines *and* His Job

(Continued from page 8)

if I tried to do everything at once. At present the road may be long and circuitous, and expensive to maintain, but it is open to traffic and the traffic is heavy and it is precious. I do not intend to disturb this traffic in the least. Whatever service the veteran was receiving from the Veterans Bureau on the day I took charge he will continue to receive. We are building from there. Such inconvenience as the reconstruction of the road may entail will be borne by the reconstruction crew—by those of us who are in the government service and whose duty it is to bear them. They will not be shifted off on to the veteran, who already has had trouble enough getting the relief he should have and for which the taxpayers are paying a good high price.

Improvement in Sixty Days

"WE will do one thing at a time. We will not cut out a single curve or angle in the old road until we have the new short-cut ready to stand all the traffic that comes that way. When will the new road be completed? Well, I am not strong on predictions. Predicting is a greatly crowded occupation, but, subject to correction, I would say that within sixty days there will have been considerable improvement.

"This bureau operated under regulations and under laws. I can change regulations. I can change them to suit my conception of how things should be done, but I cannot change the laws. I can recommend changes and I can go before Congress and urge them. Congress does not meet until December. When that time comes I will have things in hand. I will know just what laws I want changed, just how I want them changed and why. I will have had time to form matured judgment in these matters by extended observation and by consultation with others, such as officials of the Legion who have given the problems of veterans' rehabilitation very careful and very helpful study. I have no misgivings about getting from Congress what will be required to afford the best service to the veteran at the least expense to the taxpayer.

A Welcome Investigation

"I APPRECIATE, of course, that the most perfect regulations, the most adequate laws on earth, will avail little unless we have in the bureau an organization capable of administering them. Much has been said of the state of the Veterans Bureau organization before I took charge—and since, for that matter —and a good deal more, apparently, remains to be disclosed. But in this matter I must defer to the senatorial committee. It is its province; not mine. I have arranged to afford this committee every facility within my power. I am very glad this investigation will be held. I expect to profit by it greatly, and by that I mean that I expect to see that the veteran profits.

"I do not know yet just what changes will be necessary before the Veterans Bureau has an organization which will come up to the mark I have set for it,

but in sixty days—that means roughly three months after my appointment—I expect to have demonstrated a good deal. Some people may be in the wrong places. I hope they may be few in number, but few or many, they will be changed and put in the right places. And where I find that for one reason or another we cannot use the services of any individual I will be honest with that individual and honest with myself and tell him so. Inefficiency is too expensive. The people in this organization must know their jobs. This is not a training school.

"I know the organization was greatly disturbed when I came in. This unrest extended from the central office here to the districts and the sub-districts in the field. Uncertainty pervaded everything and morale was away down. This was reflected in the work of the organization. You cannot expect a man to do his best work when he is worrying about whether he will have a job tomorrow, and when the man next to him has found he can soldier on the job and get away with it. I think next week I will start on a little tour of the divisions in this office here and talk for about two minutes to the assembled personnel. I want to assure these people that industry and results will be rewarded; industry and results alone.

Not a Political Debutante

"POLITICAL pressure will not mean anything with me. I have never been in politics and I did not return to Washington at this time to make my debut. Understand me, I am not disparaging politics or political organizations. They are necessary, and there are some very effective political organizations, but the Veterans Bureau will not be one of them while I am here. And politics of another variety—office politics—will find an inhospitable soil within this organization. There will be no rings or cliques. Men and women alike will be hired, retained, advanced, transferred—in fact, their whole career with this organization will be determined by merit and merit alone. "In the employment of men veterans will be given every preference consistent with efficiency. Our problem is to rehabilitate ex-service men. Every time I hire a veteran I help myself. My problem is just that much less. Veterans will not be exempt from the high standard of efficiency required of others.

"And speaking of rehabilitating ex-service men, we have, as you know, more than 100,000 men in vocational training, a problem we have not solved satisfactorily at all. I am not prepared to say much about it at present, but we have fallen down badly on that phase of rehabilitation. Great changes must be made before we have attained what we should attain in the matter of training vocationally handicapped men for the pursuit of new occupations. But my investigation of present conditions is not complete and my plans for reform have not been made, but I want to be able to make an announcement of new policies and new procedure in this

matter for two important reasons—for the sake of the veterans who need training and for the sake of the taxpayers, as our present training expenses are heavy.

Lopping Off Expenses

"THIS bureau has been spending too much money and the veteran has had too little to show for it. Our appropriations for this fiscal year are about $450,000,000. Only a small part of this actually goes to run the bureau, however. Millions are being spent to build hospitals, to pay vocational training and disability compensation. The actual administrative expenses of the bureau were around $35,000,000 last year. But this was too much. I mean to cut those expenses down by at least $10,000,000, and I hope much more.

"Improper management is the most expensive thing in the world. When I find an organization in which the long-distance telephone and telegraph bills run high that is a pretty fair indication to me that it is a poorly-managed organization. Men have let things go, or haven't had the foresight to see them, until they have become emergencies, real or fancied, and a long-distance telephone conversation or a telegram seems necessary to do what a letter would have done in time.

"I learned that there was too much telephoning and telegraphing shortly after I came in when a field official called me from a city 2,500 miles away about a matter that should have been taken care of in a letter. I immediately issued an order limiting the use of the telephone and telegraph and these expenses have come down appreciably. In January the daily average of long distance telephone tolls for the central office was $20.91. Yesterday the charges were five cents. The average for the month is around two or three dollars.

Increased Power in Districts

"IN order to decentralize administration the Bureau is divided into fourteen regional districts, each of which is in charge of a district manager. These district managers are responsible to me and I intend that they shall be the only men outside of Washington with whom I shall deal ordinarily. I have greatly increased the responsibilities and powers of these district managers. I mean that they shall run their districts and solve their own problems, with the proper co-operation and assistance of the central office, of course. But when something goes wrong in a district the district manager cannot tell me that Sub-District Manager Smith was to blame. I will hold the district manager to blame. If Smith makes mistakes Smith should be relieved and the district manager must do the relieving. When I relieve a district worker it will be the district manager—with special exceptions, of course. In no other way can we construct an organization that will do the work the Veterans Bureau was created to do—in no other way can we eliminate the byways and detours which now make road the veteran must travel to relief so long, so unsatisfactory so expensive."

ich are General Hines's own obser-ons on a job he is pleased to call ple," though it has anything but ; reputation. But Hines means it he says. He isn't kidding any-y or trying to kid himself. He has sufficient experience with large and cult affairs to know that the most zling problems resolve themselves) a series of steps, each simple in lf. Have you ever seen a mechanic life into an automobile motor in minutes after amateurs had labored r it in vain for that many hours? a' mechanic tightens a screw here, sens one there, replaces a damaged 't somewhere else, and the engine ns again. Very simple—that is, to mechanic. Well, so it will have to with the Veterans Bureau. If the reau's difficulties prove simple of so-ion it will be because the touch of nes, the expert, make them that way. There is something about the manner which Hines speaks that inspires fidence, and there is something about quiet way of doing things that has same effect. The morale of the 'eau—of the central office in Wash-ton—has increased about one hun-ed percent since he came in, and this the face of a state of untoward condi-ns. A reorganization is under way d reorganizations are usually rough morale. Only the most capable of)rganizers can avert it. But Hines s averted it. One change at a time—e transfer, one removal, one resigna-n. So it goes, as smoothly as if it re a part of the routine—each move parently the most natural thing in e world. It seems simple. It *is* mple..

A division head told me his people ere doing almost twice as much work i they were six weeks ago. Morale as at its nadir then, and the force fell :hind with its tasks. Now you can id the workers voluntarily coming ick to their desks of evenings to :tch up.

"A new spirit has certainly taken ıld of my part of this organization," id the division chief. "We are getting ımewhere and hitting the ball. It is e old story of confidence in leader-ıip—without it no organization, I care ıt how individually capable its com-ınents may be, can be successful. I 10w I do my work a lot better. I can ı to my superiors and get decisions)w where I used to get postponements ' evasions, or be referred to someone se. Now it is 'yes' or 'no' with :asons. I am able to pass this spirit ı to those under me, and the effect is ırprising. I have never seen anything ce it since I was in the Army and itnessed the rottenest, slouchiest outfit ıat ever wore a uniform turned into crack company in two weeks, simply r changing commanding officers."

The report of another subordinate :ecutive:

"I can get more action in two hours ıan I used to get in two weeks. The ıw director certainly can distinguish :tween principles and details. He de-des on principles and the details are ɔ to us. But his instructions are usu-ly so clear that they almost indicate ıe steps necessary to carry them out." The same story comes from the rank ıd file. Work moving faster than

(*Continued on page 23*)

10-Day Tube Free

What Men Use

To get those glistening teeth

Note how many men and women show white teeth nowadays.

They are proud to show them when they smile—because they are attractive.

There is a new way of teeth cleaning which millions now employ. It means whiter, safer, cleaner teeth.

Men who want good teeth should use it. Make this free test and see just what it does.

It removes film

You can feel on your teeth a viscous film. It clings to teeth, gets between the teeth and stays. Food stains, etc., discolor it. Then it forms dingy coats. Tartar is based on film.

That's why teeth look cloudy.

Film also holds food substance which ferments and forms acids. It holds the acids in contact with the teeth to cause decay. Germs breed by millions in it, and they cause many troubles.

That's how teeth are ruined.

You must do this

Old ways of brushing do not end that film. Some always remains to threaten serious damage night and day.

So dental science sought a film com-batant, and two methods were discovered. One acts to curdle film, one to remove it.

Experts proved those ways effective. Then dentists everywhere began to advise their use.

A new-type tooth paste was created, based on modern research. The name is Pepsodent. Those two great film combatants' were embodied in it, for daily application.

Now careful people of some fifty na-tions use this new way to clean teeth.

Fights acid too

Pepsodent also multiplies the alka-linity of the saliva. That is there to neutralize mouth acids, the cause of tooth decay.

Pepsodent multiplies the starch di-gestant in the saliva. That is there to digest starch deposits on teeth which may otherwise ferment and form acids.

Those are Nature's great tooth-pro-tecting agents in the mouth. Every use of Pepsodent gives them manifold effect.

The new-day way

Pepsodent is the tooth paste of today. Millions already use it. All care-ful people will adopt it when they know its benefits.

Send the coupon for a 10-Day Tube. Note how clean the teeth feel after using. Mark the absence of the viscous film. See how teeth whiten as the film coats disappear.

Then you will realize what this method means to you, now and in the future. Cut out the coupon now.

> **Avoid Harmful Grit**
>
> Pepsodent curdles the film and removes it without harmful scouring. Its pol-ishing agent is far softer than enamel. Never use a film combatant which contains harsh grit.

BURSTS AND DUDS

Payment is made for material for this department. Unavailable manuscript returned only when accompanied by stamped envelope. Address 627 West 43d St., New York City

A. B. WALKER

ENVY

Mathematically Wrong

Private Sundodger, the most astoundingly successful evader of work the outfit had ever known, had at last through a streak of ill fortune managed to get sent out to the rifle range with the rest of the company. Naturally, all his practise having been gained by bunk fatigue his success was not sensational. In fact, he missed twenty-one shots on twenty-one chances.

"What in the sacred name of the Chinese Grenadiers is the matter with you," roared the instructor. "Can't you hit a blamed thing?"

Sundodger sought wildly for an excuse.

"'Taint my fault," he retorted. "The trouble is that the guy that set up the target didn't place it in a straight line from here."

The Homing Heart
(Sung by the Gob)

There was a lass o' Liverpool,
So like the one I knew
In gay Paree; one waits for me
In Yokohama, too.
Oh, eyes of gray are like, they say,
To tempt the best of men,
And there's a gray-eyed Boston girl
Waits till I come again.

A Scottish lassie smiled at me,
An Irish colleen, too;
The senoritas—Lotas, Nitas—
Oh, what they didn't do!
In Lisbon town are eyes of brown
That watch and weep for me:
There's room for all, and more and more,
At my broad hearth—the sea!
R. E. ALEXANDER.

The Life of Trade

There's a backwoods New England town in which the bulk of passenger traffic still goes to two competing livery stables, automobiles being yet considered tricky affairs and dangerous to fool with. The struggle

for supremacy grew keen and at last one proprietor stuck in his window a sign reading:
"Our hosses need no whip to make them go."

Next day appeared in the window of his rival the sign:
"Keerect. The wind blows them along."

Hiking Days Are Over

Fresh from the Army and looking for excitement came ex-Private Buck. He glanced over the field of opportunities and decided on a job in the police force. He didn't know, however, that nowadays cops have to pass intelligence tests and all that sort of thing.

"How far is it from New York to Pittsburg?" asked the examiner.

Buck picked up his hat.

"I don't know," he retorted with dignity and emphasis, "and what's more, if that's going to be my beat, I resign right now."

The Little Spendthrift

This one comes straight from Honolulu. A Hawaiian took his son, Akana, to the theater and the pair took seats in the front row of the gallery. The play was a thrilling melodrama of the old-style type and grew so exciting that the boy, leaning further and further over the rail, finally lost his balance and plunged down.

In much agitation his father peered into the darkened depths.

"Akana, Akana!" he bellowed. "For the love of Heaven come back! It costs a dollar down there!"

In Punkin Falls

Stranger: "Who is that fellow over in the corner of the post office making so much noise?"

Native: "Oh, that's only old Jed Turner. He's harmless. He's just talking to himself."

Stranger: "What? All that racket and just talking to himself?"

Native: "Well, you see, he's mighty hard of hearing."

Unofficial Medical Guide

STALLITIS: A congenital disease, afflicting those who are born tired. The ailment is very infectious and should be confined (with the patient) lest it spread to others in the camp. Attacks usually come just previous to reveille, long hikes or maneuvers.

The most effective remedy, devised by Major Howe I. Torture, U. S. M. C., is as follows: Tap the patient's knees with a sledgehammer for nerve reflex, test him for paralysis by attempting to make a human pin cushion of him, revive him with a pail of ice-cold water and take a blood test, using the largest spike obtainable. Inform the patient that while his condition is not now alarming it may easily develop to the state where the removal of the tonsils, the appendix, adenoids and left leg will become necessary and that he is to report any new symptoms. His complete recovery will date from that moment.

A Weighty Problem

The tragedian, whose success had not been startling, had just signed a contract to tour South Africa and Australia. Exultantly he told a friend of it, but the latter shook his head dismally.

"The ostrich," he explained in a pitying tone, "lays an egg weighing anywhere from two to four pounds."

The Earmarks of a Dirty Crack

Two juvenile inhabitants of Brickdust Row, where tempers are higher than social standing, were having an altercation.

"Yah!" taunted one. "Yer mother takes in washin'!"

"Wot if she does?" countered the other. "Yer didn't suppose she'd leave it hangin' out over night unless yer father was in prison, did yer?"

Modesty

The lady had the eye of a bargain-hunter. She bustled up to the young clerk lounging against the nearest counter in the men's furnishing department and demanded:

"I'd like to see the smartest thing you have in men's clothing."

"What time would you care to have me meet you?" he asked with perfect poise.

Viewpoints au Naturel

"St. Patrick's Day falls in the middle of March as usual," mused the American.

"And will be celebrated in the muddle of Ireland," added the Englishman.

"In spite of the meddle of England," concluded the son of Erin.

An Important Member

Sally Brown's big, husky son had joined the Army, and one of her neighbors asked how he was getting along.

"Dat boy of mine," she answered proudly, "mus' be one of de mostest impo'tant members of de hull Army, kaze dey never let him go nowheres lessen he has a guard with him."

Sensible View

Mrs. Tiff: "I never until now realized that I married a man without an atom of sense."

Mr. Tiff: "My dear, how on earth could you possibly have married any other kind?"

City Notice

Ding, dong, dell. Pussy's in the well. Notify the Board of Health. They'll protect the commonwealth.

How Would You Figure It?

"So you think the pretty new school teacher likes you. What makes you think so?"

"Well, when I call on her in the evening and get ready to go, she orders me to stay in half an hour longer for not behaving."

No Surgical Enthusiasm

Pat's finger had been caught in a buzz saw and hacked completely off. He was rushed to a doctor.

"Was it cut off clean that way all at once?" asked the M.D.

"Sure," retorted Pat with some sarcasm, "ye don't think I held it there just to make a good job of it, do ye?"

"For real underwear value give me Dollar Topkis"

"TALK about getting my money's worth in Topkis—I'd pay double and not kick.

"Even without such good quality fabrics, I'd still get a big dollar's worth in the comfort Topkis gives my body."

Dollar Topkis is roomy all over. Large arm-holes. Extra wide, extra long legs.

Full size always guaranteed. First quality nainsook and other high-grade fabrics. Preshrunk—to keep full size.

Topkis wears and wears. Seams closely stitched—buttons sewed on securely.

No good dealer will ask more than One Dollar for the Topkis Men's Union Suit—but they'll say it's worth more.

Men's Shirts and Drawers, 75c a garment. 75c for Boys' Union Suits. Girls' Bloomer Union Suits, and Children's Waist Union Suits.

In Canada, Men's Union Suits $1.50.

New illustrated booklet will teach you what's what about underwear. It's free. Send postal for it today.

TOPKIS BROTHERS COMPANY, Wilmington, Delaware

General Sales Offices: 350 Broadway, New York City

Ask for TOPKIS Underwear　　　　　　　　*Look for the Topkis label*

Athletic　　　TOPKIS　　　Underwear

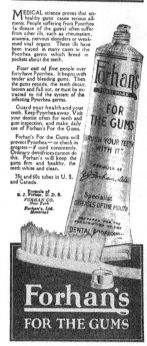

Keeping Step with the Legion

Boys, Generals, Mothers

DID you know there's going to be an International Boys' Week from April 29th to May 5th? Well, there is. It is a week during which sponsors of the movement hope to encourage every phase of boy-welfare work. Posts that have adopted Boy Scout troops may see an opportunity in this.

By the way, Boys' Week will begin just two days after the 101st anniversary of the birthday of General U. S. Grant, which falls on April 27th. And, also by the way, it will close just two weeks before this year's celebration of Mother's Day—May 13th.

Right Off the Bat

THE Step Keeper was poring over some letters the other day when the door opened and in came two Legionnaires from West Alexandria, Ohio. They had come to see the director of the National Legion Film Service, but they thought they'd also like a look at the National Headquarters Bureau of the Weekly. They were B. F. Bowman and G. A. Shell, members of James E. Ryan Post.

"Are you the Step Keeper?" remarked one. We nodded modestly.

"You say you want to learn interesting things about posts that have put on movies? Maybe we two can tell you something."

They did. Here's it:

West Alexandria is a town of maybe a thousand people. James E. Ryan Post can never have more than sixty-five or seventy members. But we've gone into the movie business and today we're the biggest entertainers in West Alexandria. Our post makes about twenty dollars a week net profit and we're cutting prices on our shows so the people won't have to furnish us so much profit.

When we first decided to go into the movie business we discovered that the public school auditorium was the best place for exhibiting. It seats about six hundred people. The school board said we could have the use of the auditorium if we would let them use our equipment for educational pictures on occasion. So we went into business as guests of the school board.

We have been using satisfactory machines, but now we're here to talk over buying two new ones; they'll cost about $725 all told: they'll be worth it. When we started out we advertised in the local paper. This got us the good will of the owner. We gave him tickets so he could review our shows and he gives us "readers" in exchange. All that is legitimate advertising.

We decided that what movies we had would be good movies. We made our first purchases after considerable discussion in the post. Now, after every entertainment the post puts on, members get together in meeting and discuss how the feature picture went and make suggestions for future bookings. Also, we have censors. We asked the censors to serve; we didn't want people to criticize our shows adversely while it was within our power to avoid such criticism, so we asked the mayor, a minister and the superintendent of schools to serve as our board of censors.

Are our shows successful? We'll say they are. We give one a week, and our average attendance is five hundred. We charge twenty cents for adults and fifteen cents for children. We've got the movie business on such a substantial scale that it is hard to conceive of anybody coming to town and opening a rival show that could compete with us. We have given the town its money's worth. Once a month we give prizes to the boy and the girl having the best school records in town. As we said, we pay for the advertising space in the local paper; we didn't want to ask a gift on a money-making venture like ours. At every show we get out a twelve-page program. Local merchants are glad to advertise in this. It is not only a program for the show we are running, but an advertisement of future exhibitions. The program pays for itself and makes a little profit beside.

The movie finances are kept separate from the post finances up to the time when the profits are taken out and put into the post treasury, when they cease to be part of the movie enterprise. On some of the money the post plans to offer movies at future post meetings; this will stimulate attendance, we think. We plan to give a dinner Friday night (you ought to come over) to the Chamber of Commerce. We're going to show them "Flashes of Action." Such a picture ought to solidify our position with the town, although our shows have been such a benefit themselves that there's no question in our town but that The American Legion is a doggone fine organization working constantly to make America, and particularly West Alexandria, a better place to live in.

That is one of the principal benefits of staging a movie. It helps the town appreciate the Legion. Pretty soon we're going to put on "The Man Without a Country," which the movie director has been telling us about. That ought to be splendid Americanism work.

A little later the movie director sent for the Ohio delegation—probably to try to sell them something or other—so the Step Keeper missed out on further information about conducting movie shows. But it was only a short time after that before a letter came in from Dave Kemper, commander of George H. Hockett Post of Anderson, Indiana, which contained still further information along the same line. And here's that:

For the benefit of Legion posts that have never put over a successful motion picture show, I would like to have a few lines of your valuable space to tell how we exploited and exhibited the Legion film, "The Man Without a Country," try."

Anderson is a city of 30,000. We arranged with the owner of the best motion picture theatre in the city to turn his house over to us for four days on the following basis: We allowed him his usual house expense, including advertising and overhead, and receipts above that expense were divided equally between the theatre and the post. Half of the post's profits were sent to National Headquarters as a rental for the film. I believe it is better for the post, wherever possible, to rent the theatre outright. This arrangement makes it unnecessary to divide profits with the owner.

We started our exploitation campaign with an announcement in the newspapers. This was clipped from the press sheet sent to us from the Film Service at National Headquarters. We sent out a circular letter to every telephone subscriber announcing the exhibition of "The Man Without a Country" and attaching a reservation blank to be used in reserving tickets. We distributed tickets to members of the post and its Auxiliary unit, each member being asked to sell five.

About a week before the first exhibition date we sent out our "wrecking crew" with a bunch of automobile windshield stickers. These were pasted on every automobile in sight and it wasn't long before we had everybody talking about "The Man Without a Country." Then the members of the Auxiliary unit agreed to call up every telephone subscriber requesting him to see the picture.

Two days before the show we arranged with a bank to offer a prize to students of Anderson for the best essay on the Patriotism inspired by the photoplay "The Man Without a Country." The bank announced the contest in paid advertisements in the newspapers. The prize offered was a ten-dollar gold piece.

On the day preceding the first exhibition the mayor issued a statement calling on every citizen who could to see "The Man Without a Country."

Our first evening show started with a packed house and everyone who saw the picture praised it. This favorable comment brought out large audiences on the following nights. The newspapers printed favorable reviews.

In addition to the feature program, we used the comedy "O Promise Me," a two-reel educational side-splitter produced by members of Hollywood Post of the Legion. This comedy can be obtained through the Film Service or from the Educational Exchanges at a rental of $5 a day.

I forgot to say that we gave a private screening of "The Man Without a Country" film for the ministers and school officials of the city, which resulted in the ministers announcing the picture favorably from the pulpits.

Fourth Division This Way!

MEN of the Ivy Division, attention! The Fourth Division Association, through the agency of the Legion Library, is offering to former members of the outfit and their friends "The History of the Fourth Division"—370 pages full of facts from the time of organization and the training period, through the Aisne-Marne, St. Mihiel and Meuse Argonne Offensives, the days of occupation in Germany, to the return home. Sixty pages of illustrations, the Honor Roll, authentic maps, lists of awards of decorations, are all included in the volume, which is being offered at two dollars a copy.

"The History of the Twenty-Ninth Division"—just another reminder to the Blue and Gray men that now is their chance to get a copy of their division's history. The price is five dollars.

All orders with remittance should be sent to the Legion Library, 627 West 43d Street, New York City.

A Golden Opportunity to Help Your Buddies

Sale of Poppies This Year Will Build Up Thousands of Post Treasuries

Price
4½c each
Delivered

IN MEMORIAM

Your post needs money to carry on relief work among disabled buddies. Your post needs money for its quota of the Graves Endowment Fund. National Headquarters of the Legion has a plan whereby the 17,000 Legion and Auxiliary Posts can raise these funds. And there is a true spirit of helpfulness back of this campaign which should ensure the hearty co-operation of your entire post membership.

National Headquarters has procured a large quantity of high grade silk Poppies, made by French disabled men and their dependents. These artificial flowers are of a decidedly superior quality entirely in keeping with the dignity of the American Legion. Any profits that might be derived by National Headquarters from the sale of these Poppies will be devoted entirely to relief and service work. If your post has delayed taking definite action on this plan, call a special meeting at once. You still have time to fulfill the post obligation to the dead and disabled. Estimate the number of poppies that will be required and place your order immediately with National Headquarters. Shipments will be made promptly, C.O.D., or if preferred, your remittance in full can be included with the order. Use the coupon for your order blank.

Remember—MEMORIAL DAY IS POPPY DAY THROUGHOUT THE AMERICAN LEGION.

All Poppy transactions cash. No charge or approval orders accepted.

**Emblem Division
National Headquarters**

The American Legion
Indianapolis, Indiana

Emblem Division,
Nat'l Hqrs.
The American Legion
Indianapolis, Ind.

Enclosed is $..............
for which please send.........
poppies. □ Check here if
wanted sent c. o. d.

Name ....

Address ....

Post.....................................
....

Wanted: $100,000 by May 30

(Continued from page 10)

cago: **40 and 8 Society, $100;** Richard J. Glaser, $5; *Maywood:* Marion L. Humphrey, $5; *Quincy:* Harry W. Phillips, $1.

INDIANA. *Indianapolis:* **Hayward-Barcus Auxiliary, $10;** C. J. Harris, $2; *Michigan City:* Clarence J. Peters, $1; *Wanatah:* D. L. Faurote, $2; *Rochester:* **Leroy C. Shelton Post, $5.**

IOWA. *Randalia:* H. J. Holems, $5; *Rock Rapids:* Ex-28th Infantryman, $2.

KANSAS. *Burdick:* Wesley L. Freedlum, $2; *Council Grove:* Ralph S. Kendle, $1. *Winfield:* William Canton, $1.

KENTUCKY. *Paducah:* **Chief Paduke Post, $25.**

MASSACHUSETTS. *Boston:* Overseas Nurse, $1; *Chester:* Legionnaire, $5; *Fairhaven:* **Auxiliary to Fairhaven Post, $10;** *Medfield:* **Beckwith Post, $5;** *Wakefield:* H. C. Bennett, $1.

MICHIGAN. *Alpena:* **William F. Weine Post, $5;** *Detroit:* J. Colston, $1; J. Davidson, $1; R. Fipel, $5; E. Hagerstrom, $1; D. G. Jones, $1; J. E. Murray, $2.50; *Grand Rapids:* **Carl A. Johnson Post, $1,000;** *Rives Junction:* R. G. Woodard, $1; *Wyandotte:* Edward C. Headman Post, $10.

MINNESOTA. *East Grand Forks:* A. R. Restadius, $5; *Virginia:* **J. Burt Pratt Post, $10;** *Windom:* **Auxiliary to Windom Post, $1.**

MISSISSIPPI. *Clarksdale:* Lester C. Franklin, $1; *Corinth:* W. C. Adams, $1; **Perry A. Johns Post, $5;** R. B. Moore, $1; E. J. Duncan, $1; B. L. Collins, $1; Elmore Jobe, $1; Nelson Timlake, $1; Edwin Ajax, $1; Joe Reighardt, $2; C. W. Norwood, $1; H. G. Peerey, $1; G. C. Taylor, Jr., $1; Albert T. Ajax, $1; R. G. Redding, $1; Jeff D. Harris, $2; D. K. Fyfe, $1; J. M. Kimmons, $1; W. G. Kimmons, $1; M. F. Rubel, $1; A. S. Rubel, $1; W. W. King, $1; N. L. Armistead, $1; T. P. Holman, $1; N. S. Sweat, $1; D. Mercier, $1; Myrlin McCullar, $1; S. D. Bramlitt, $1; Lloyd Graham, $1; Jameson C. Jones, $1; M. H. McRae, $1; J. R. Peters, $1; J. M. Powell, $1; *Greenwood:* **Post No. 29, $19.95;** *Jackson:* John B. Hudson, $1; *Laurel:* Ambrose Schauber,

$1; *McComb:* Kenneth G. Price, $1; **Magnolia Post, $9.**

MISSOURI. *Windsor:* R. J. Jennings, $2; *St. Louis:* **Post No. 433, $11.**

MONTANA. *Bozeman:* R. B. Millen, $10; *Havre:* **Havre Post, $5.**

NEBRASKA. *Lincoln:* **Lincoln Post, $50;** *Omaha:* **Douglas County Post, $38.08;** *Ponca:* Carl Scheffel, $2.

NEW HAMPSHIRE. *Keene:* O. E. Cain, $10.

NEW JERSEY. *Bridgeton:* J. Irving Moore, $2; *Elizabeth:* **Argonne Post, $7.**

NEW YORK. *Brooklyn:* John Watson, $1; *Buffalo:* Walter A. Schutrum, $1; *Piermont:* E. F. Lewis, $1; *S. Glens Falls:* **Mohican Post, $10;** *Syracuse:* Mrs. Willard E. Lape, $1; *Westport:* **Lasher-Still Post, $10.**

NORTH DAKOTA. *Dunseith:* Milton B. Miles, $1; Gene Olstad, $1; Allan Trotter, $1; Ethel Stanford, $1; Carl Bopsted, $1; George M. Carlson, $1; Herman B. Serwin, $1; *Heaton:* Lester C. Nichols, $5.

OHIO. *Akron:* Constant Southworth, $5; *Pandora:* C. D. La Rue, $2.

OKLAHOMA. *Braggs:* **Claude Pierce Post, $2.50;** *Oklahoma City:* **Auxiliary to Oklahoma City Post, $15.**

OREGON. *Redmond:* **Ray Johnson Post, $10;** *Ukiah:* W. B. Byrne, $1.

PENNSYLVANIA. *Allentown:* Ralph E. Fry, $5; *Folsom:* J. A. Palen, $2; *Hepburnville:* B. A. Johnson, $1; *Kittanning:* Henry C. Colwell, $5; *Lancaster:* **Auxiliary to Lancaster Post, $15;** *Leechburg:* Horace H. Trimble, $1; *North Brighton:* Harold G. Engle, $1; *Philadelphia:* Walter D. Roach, $1; Robert F. Wright, $1; *State College:* Anonymous, $2.

SOUTH CAROLINA. *Aiken:* J. W. Ashhurst, Jr., $1.

TEXAS. *Freeport:* Dr. W. N. Shaw, $1.

VERMONT. *Proctor:* John H. Litch, $1.

WASHINGTON. *Ferndale:* **Kulshan Post, $10;** *Yakima:* Ralph D. Craig, $1.

WISCONSIN. *Milwaukee:* Dr. Edwin Henes, Jr., $1.

WYOMING. *Sheridan:* **John D. Garbutt Post, $50;** *Worland:* H. J. Brandt, $2.

For pleasure or utility

—the opportunities for selling motorcycles are equally great.

While the motorcycle is bought largely for pleasure, the demand for business purposes is increasing tremendously.

Congested traffic and limited parking facilities present growing problems for ordinary automotive delivery.

INDIAN Scout Service Car is the answer for business deliveries. Its small size and quick pick up send it *through* traffic. It parks in *between* autos. Low cost and maintenance make it most economical.

INDIAN Scout and Big Chief 74 are the popular motorcycles in the pleasure field—we haven't dealers enough to take care of the demand.

We offer good territory for INDIAN dealers

Mail the coupon and get our free book, "The INDIAN Dealer's Franchise"

Hendee Mfg. Co., Dept. L, Springfield, Mass.

Name..............................

Street..............................

Town................State............

Present Occupation ....

Age............

Indian Motocycle

The Facts of the Japanese Question

(Continued from page 11)

his service in the Japanese army or navy. Several thousand Japanese children are added by birth to the population of this country every year, but the report of the California Board of Control has the word of the Japanese vice-consul at San Francisco that not more than a dozen Japanese children have signed this document; and so far as could be learned none of these had been accepted by the Tokio government.

"But how about the American-born Japanese children?" asks the man who lives three thousand miles from the Pacific Coast. "Don't they get a thoroughly American point of view in the American schools?"

Perhaps; but they also get the Japanese point of view in Japanese schools in this country or, if their parents can afford it, in Japan.

The Japanese say that the purpose of these schools is simply to acquaint children with the Japanese language, so that they may talk with their parents. They say that the original text books, brought from Japan, are being revised to eliminate much that would be unfamiliar to American-born Japanese children. On the other hand there is the testimony of Congressman Siegel who said, during a congressional investigation:

The other day we went to see one of the schools and we saw the book and all we saw in it was a series of pictures showing the success of the Japanese forces, and we looked through the entire school book, the book from which they were being taught, and we could not find anything in

these about the United States, either by picture or otherwise.

So much for the training of some Japanese children. Others fare more interestingly; they are sent to Japan to complete their education. An examination of the records of the San Francisco immigration office, conducted by the Japanese Exclusion League of California, indicated that during a period of three years 6,649 Japanese children were sent to Japan. As the average period of stay is six years, it is estimated that between ten and fifteen thousand children from California alone are now in that country. It may seem difficult to reconcile these foregoing evidences of clannishness, of solidarity, with the Japanese attitude toward intermarriage; but actually it fits smoothly into place when you remember that they appear to regard the Pacific Coast as a province of the Mikado. They are an astute people, the Japanese, and they are looking a long way ahead. Their newspapers and their spokesmen frequently refer to a "plan of one hundred years," which is supposed to mean the time when they will assert their numerical supremacy in those Pacific Coast States which they seem to have picked for their own. If Japanese wives are not numerous enough to accomplish this purpose, then—but let me quote from an editorial in the *Shin Sekai* of San Francisco:

Even if not a single Japanese woman comes it is not possible to prevent the seed of our great Yamato race being sown on the American continent by marriages with

Americans, with French, with Indians and with Negroes, especially since there are already 100,000 Japanese here and 5,000 born annually. Supposing that we Japanese were prohibited from owning or cultivating the land. Even the laws of California are not forever unchangeable. The day will come when the real strength of the Japanese will make a clean sweep of all laws.

There is a bombastic sound about that last sentence, but it is not entirely disregarded on the Pacific Coast. In another generation the Japanese will dominate Hawaii by sheer force of numbers. What is to prevent that disciplined, prolific people from accomplishing the same result elsewhere in course of time?

Yes, all this has a bombastic sound, but similar sounds came out of Germany not so long ago, and one day we discovered that they muffled the rumble of gun carriages. It is the opinion of the Legion's National Oriental Committee that the Japanese look forward to a conquest, peaceable or otherwise, of the Pacific Coast, though their aspirations for the time being would be satisfied, it is believed, if they were admitted to this country on the same terms as other races and were accorded all social and political rights, including that of unrestricted marriage.

How the Pacific Coast will finally adjust its differences with the Japanese within the country to the satisfaction of both parties, perhaps even the Pacific Coast does not know. A law preventing intermarriage is advocated, but that sounds as improbable as wholesale deportation. In the broader views of the question there is hope in an exclusion act which will work. Whatever is undertaken, the Japanese government must join with the United States in a spirit of cooperation. The settlement of the question is in the interest of both countries. The uncompromising attitude of the Pacific Coast and the persistently aggressive attitude of the Japanese will cause serious trouble when the economic pressure on the two races becomes too strong. It is, as the National Oriental Committee says, time to be frank. The Japanese are a first-class people, but they must not be allowed to absorb the Pacific Coast.

That Man Hines

(Continued from page 17)

ever before. The new boss is the goods. So, all in all, it looks like a fine start. So far, so good—in fact, excellent. But it is well that General Hines himself reminds us that predictions are apt to cause woe. Otherwise we might be tempted to go a little bit further.

It is time, however, that we were looking into the service record of this man Hines who is able to transform the most puzzling of tasks into "simple" undertakings. Well, he was born in Salt Lake City in 1879. His father was an engineer who had gone West some years before to prospect in the gold mines. Young Hines was brought up in mining camps and he caught the fever early. When he finished high school he went to the Utah Agricultural College, which happened to give a good course in mining engineering. Frank already had acquired some practical ex-

ALONG THE FRENCH HIGHWAYS

you passed little "lavoirs" where the peasants gathered on wash day. On the grassy hills lay the white garments drying in the sunshine. They looked cool and comfortable to you, who perhaps tugged to loosen the collar of a sticky blouse. The GORDON, an ARROW shirt, is just a little more comfortable and better made than shirts on "the beaten path." It's built of pure and permanently white Oxford. Get into one.

They're a step forward in comfort—and are suited for light or heavy marching order.

$3.00

With attached collar made by the makers of ARROW Collars. The cuffs are buttoned, or of the French model.

GORDON *an* ARROW SHIRT

CLUETT, PEABODY & CO., INC.

perience about mines. Since he was old enough to push a dump car he had been at it, and after that he had experimented with a cyanide process of reducing gold.

The fledgling engineer was in his second year at college when we went to war with Spain, and Frank went along. He went as a private in Battery B of the Utah Light Artillery. Battery B went to the Philippines. Hines became a corporal, a sergeant, then first sergeant. He participated in twenty-two engagements and was recommended for a Congressional Medal of Honor for heroism in the attack on Manila, when he led a relieving force to two guns on the beach which were in danger of capture. In March of 1899 Sergeant Hines again distinguished himself on the field in the assault of Malolos, capital of the insurgent leader Aguinaldo, and was promoted to a second lieutenancy on the spot.

Battery B came home the next year, but Lieutenant Hines decided to stay with the Army. He passed the examinations for a commission in the Regular service, when the enlightening discovery was made that for a year Hines had held his lieutenancy in the volunteers in violation of law. He was not yet twenty-one years old. In the assault on Malolos they had not stopped to inquire the age of Sergeant Hines, then only 19. So Hines waited a year and in 1901 received his second lieutenancy in the coast artillery, Regular Army.

In June of 1914, when he was a captain, he obtained a leave and was sent to Greece by the Bethlehem Steel Corporation as technical advisor on coast defenses to the Greek government. On the outbreak of the war Hines was recalled to active duty and sent to Italy to assist in returning to the United States tourists and refugees who were caught in the embattled countries. Under the direction of the American ambassador at Rome Captain Hines established a base at Naples and chartered and fitted out ships in which 3,100 American citizens were sent home in two months. For this service he was highly commended by the State Department.

This chance service may have been the turning point in his career. The organizing ability he had displayed on that occasion was deemed of more worth to the Army than the valor he had displayed in twenty-two battles in the Philippines. Executive genius is rare among military leaders. Major General Harbord, chief of the S. O. S. in France, and the foremost executive of the war, once remarked to Colonel Franklin D'Olier, after he had inspected one of the latter's depots, that "it is comparatively easy to find men who can lead regiments; this is the work the Army finds hard to get done." So when we got in the war Captain Hines was sent to Hoboken as chief of staff of the port of embarkation. His ability attracted immediate attention. He was promoted rapidly, becoming a brigadier general and chief of the Embarkation Service in eight months. The dispatch without mishap of 2,082,000 troops overseas in eighteen months was one of the wonders of the war, and the man who organized and directed this effort from first to last was General Hines.

In August of 1918 General Hines accompanied the Secretary of War

abroad and during September of that year he appeared with the Secretary before the Inter-Allied Transport Council at London and dickered with the British to obtain an additional allotment of British tonnage for American troops and cargo. In 1919 he returned to Europe and negotiated with British and French officials, the meeting resulting in a settlement of the transport accounts of those governments against the United States on a basis exceptionally favorable to the United States. While abroad he also made arrangements to bring into War Department service additional vessels to hurry the homesick A. E. F. back to the States.

These were all feats that called for executive genius of a high order. General Hines is one of the few officers who received both the Army and Navy Distinguished Service Medal. The King of England gave him the Order of the Bath, which seems to be an evidence of the sporting qualities of the British, for General Hines got our men taken to France in British ships for $81.75 a head, or half what the British shipowners wanted to charge. The General also has the French Legion of Honor and numerous other foreign decorations, and the Utah Agricultural College conferred upon him the diploma he had failed to receive twenty years before when he went off to fight the Spaniards.

In August of 1920 General Hines resigned from the Army to become the manager of a trans-Atlantic shipping company. This was the job he left to try to put the Veterans Bureau on its feet. The general is a charter member of George Washington Post No. 1 of The American Legion, Washington, D. C., the first post to receive its national charter—it was called John J. Pershing Post at first but the St. Louis caucus in 1919 decided that no post should be named for a living person. The general now holds his membership in Edward M. MacKee Post of Whitestone, Long Island, where he lives—and he paid his dues for 1923 long ago.

To Batch or Not to Batch

(Continued from page 9)

a summer," Jimson objected, "and one marvel of an Auxiliary unit doesn't necessarily prove that the same shower of blessings will miraculously descend on every Legion post that gives up its bachelor independence."

"Well, all I can say," declared Doggett, "is that from what I can gather about the doings of the Auxiliary all over the country—my wife, being an enthusiastic member, keeps me well posted—they average a pretty high percentage of efficiency and helpfulness. Do you know, I rather figure that the services rendered by the Legion Auxiliary closely parallel the work done by the women in the various wartime auxiliary organizations. First of all, they assist in the activities of the Legion and back us up in whatever we want to do, just as the Y girls and the Salvation Army lassies helped us keep us going at top speed when we were chasing the Boches. Next, their looking out for the welfare of disabled veterans is right in line with the hospital service of the army nurses and of the Red

Behold the Kaiser as a Thing of Shame!

Here at last is the powerful, graphic picture of the Kaiser's private, secret life—of his birth, his strange disease, his power, his degraded court favorites, his ghastly dissipations, his terrible utterances—and finally his exile!

Here is the man that made the earth tremble—stripped bare of the trappings of Empire—brought face to face with the evidence of his amazing sins against Heaven and man! The searing light of truth has found the dark spot in his soul, revealing his most hideous crimes.

Here at last is the *whole* truth about William Hohenzollern—the astounding truth that has shocked nobles of the German Court and is making the entire world gasp!

To miss one word of these exposures is to miss the most astounding revelation of our age!

NOW PUBLISHED ~ The World Astounding-Exposé!

"Behind the Scenes with the Kaiser"

By the Baroness von Larisch of the Imperial Household

There was one person in this world who saw the Kaiser in his innermost private life—who heard his secret thoughts uttered aloud—who witnessed his strange intimacies, his whims, his desires—who knew him as no one has ever dreamed of knowing the Kaiser—and that person was the Baroness von Larisch of the Imperial Household!

"Behind the Scenes with the Kaiser," the revelations which astounded the various nobles of the German Court itself, are the result of the private papers and diaries kept by the Baroness

during her long stay in the Imperial Household.

She pledged herself to tell the "truth, the whole truth and nothing but the truth." In carrying out her pledge she reveals phases of the ex-Monarch's character and life which, but for her writings, would be lost to the world—would die with the exile himself.

But, as these amazing disclosures are now sure to live, a sensationally large edition of these volumes has been published. The public rush to obtain this set of two volumes will be unprecedented in the history of book publishing! The amazingly low price of $2.48 for the two-volume set insures a tremendous demand.

Be prompt in getting your set! There probably never will be anything like these startling revelations published again in *your lifetime*. And the time to read them is *NOW*—while the Kaiser is attempting his own astounding defence.

What Famous Editors Say:

A Daring Writer
"As written as no man ever dared write before. Behind it is a real barometer. Lady - in - waiting. This lady was long in the service of the Kaiser and knows, therefore, of what she speaks so freely."—New York World.

Better than Pepys
"Honest What's that but keeping the Court Marshall's instructions in mind? If any reader imagines that the Allhighest court is high-minded or that William is a statesman twenty-four hours in every day, let him read these volumes. There is enough in them for a lifetime."—St. Louis Post Dispatch.

The Curious Gratified
The craving for the most private sort of knowledge regarding royalty finds abundant gratification in these Secret Court Memoirs."—Brooklyn Citizen.

Was the "spook-hunt" staged to leave the Kaiser alone with the Countess Fritz?

How did the Kaiser keep the Empress locked up when he went in quest of pleasure?

What did the Kaiser ask "Daisy," the German beauty, to do for him in London?

Was official sanction enjoyed by 14-year-old German nobles who kept mistresses?

What was contained in the anonymous letters to the Kaiser that scandalized the German court?

What was the conversation between the Kaiser and the actress, Rosa Poppe, behind the scenes on the stage of the Royal Play House which made the actress exclaim: "I must beg leave from your Majesty. The part I am playing tonight does not admit of frivolities."

What did the little Dutch girl do to the Kaiser in exile?

The Baroness von Larisch has some absorbingly interesting answers to these startling questions.

Send No Money

It is not necessary to send money. Merely mail the coupon and the two-volume set will go forward at once. When the books arrive, deposit $2.48 plus postage, with the postman, and the set is yours. If you are not satisfied with the books, return them within five days and your money will be refunded. But you must act now, before the edition is exhausted. Send no money; just mail the coupon.

HERTAG PUBLISHING CORPORATION
Dept. 64 2 West 29th Street, New York City

Cross. Then the aid given by the Auxiliary to war orphans and to the families of ex-service men in financial difficulties is just the kind of help the Red Cross and other organizations gave the families of soldiers and sailors while we were in service. What do you say? Does the parallel hold?"

"Certainly seems to," I said.

"You make out a pretty good case," Jimson grudgingly admitted.

"My argument," continued Doggett, "is that an Auxiliary unit is just as helpful to a Legion post to-day as the war service organizations were to the Army and Navy back in 1917 and 1918. Take the question of eats alone. I can testify—and both of you can, too—that after wandering around in the mud and cold up near the front it felt mighty good to happen on a Salvation Army dugout and get a cup of coffee. I tell you it brings back the old times when the Auxiliary members serve refreshments after a post meeting. And then there's the matter of decorating the clubrooms. I guess you'll agree that women have better taste than men and know how to fix a place up so as to make it attractive and comfortable-looking. I can remember how good the interiors of some Red Cross and K. of C. and Y huts looked to me after days in the trenches or in lousy billets. Our Auxiliary has helped us a lot to make our headquarters look more home-like and less barn-like."

"Sure, by tying a pink silk ribbon on every chair," Jimson snorted.

"Gosh, Jim, you certainly have an ingrowing grouch," Doggett said indulgently. "You need the influence of some woman to civilize you. But to get back to the main argument, there are a hundred and one ways in which it can and does directly help the Legion post. Raising funds, serving eats, co-operating in entertainments, giving dances and other social affairs, participating in the celebration of patriotic holidays, stirring up Legionnaires to active interest and continuous attendance, fixing up the clubrooms, supporting the Legion in resolutions and letters aimed at misguided law-makers—you could make a list as long as you please of the various ways Auxiliary units have helped Legion posts. So much for that.

"When you come to what the Auxiliary does for the veterans in hospitals, then you hit what I think is their most important job, at least at present. I know that when I was in the hospital at Neuilly nothing did more to keep me cheered up than the nurses in the ward and the women of the auxiliary organizations who came to visit us. Think of the rotten luck of the doughboys who are still—after four years—tied to a hospital bed. How they must welcome any change in the monotony of their lives! Whenever there's a veterans' hospital in or near a town with a Legion post the Legionnaires ought to make it a point to visit the out-of-luck buddies regularly and often.

"But most of us are working so darn hard to earn enough to pay our own way that we don't get much time to go visiting. Consequently, it's up to our wives and mothers and sisters to substitute for us—in other words, the Auxiliary. And they do it. In almost every veterans' hospital in the country you'll find some Auxiliary unit with a motherly eye on the comfort of the dis-

Past Performances

Just glance over the report of standing of departments in the Weekly subscription card race of 1923 and compare the standing of your department with its position last year. Note that the five leaders this year occupied the 16th, 35th, 48th, 23rd and 21st places, respectively, last year. If your department is included in this group of go-getters, pat yourself on the back for having helped place it there—and keep on working. If, however, it is one not up to or above its last year's record, that's a signal for YOU and your post to step on it and sign up your backward members. The April 4th standing of departments in proportion of 1923 cards received to total 1922 membership, with the standing on the same date last year, based on the previous year's ratio, follows:

1923		1922	1923		1922
1	Georgia	16	25	Colorado	41
2	Idaho	35	26	Washington	47
3	Arizona	48	27	Wisconsin	12
4	N. Hampshire	23	28	Connecticut	43
5	S. Dakota	21	29	Texas	28
6	Nebraska	6	30	Ohio	11
7	S. Carolina	33	31	Tennessee	24
8	Iowa	7	32	Oklahoma	3
9	Illinois	34	33	Alabama	30
10	New York	38	34	Delaware	46
11	Arkansas	2	35	Montana	36
12	Maine	25	36	Massachusetts	40
13	Indiana	18	37	Virginia	37
14	Rhode Island	14	38	Maryland	27
15	Kansas	26	39	Kentucky	19
16	N. Jersey	44	40	Mississippi	20
17	Minnesota	10	41	Michigan	32
18	Utah	4	42	Wyoming	15
19	N. Dakota	13	43	Oregon	22
20	Vermont	29	44	N. Carolina	9
21	Penna.	17	45	Florida	1
22	W. Virginia	42	46	D. of C.	31
23	Nevada	49	47	Missouri	8
24	California	39	48	N. Mexico	5
		49	Louisiana	45

bled men. They bring cookies, fruits, jellies, all kinds of good eatables not apt to be overabundant on a hospital menu. They furnish magazines, books, radios, phonographs, entertainment, clothes; they help in straightening out compensation claims—every sort of service that the hospitalized veteran needs.

"And when there are no hospitals containing ex-service men within easy reach, then the Auxiliary often goes out of its way to contribute good things to the men who have paid and are paying the heaviest price for our victory. For instance, I remember reading that out in Nevada, there being no soldiers in hospitals in the State, the Auxiliary sends ten dozen cookies a week over the mountains to veterans in California hospitals. One idea that many Auxiliary units have adopted and followed up is making sure that disabled men who enlisted from the local community are taken care of, no matter where they are hospitalized. The men appreciate the personal interest of people from the home town, you can bet. Perhaps the Auxiliary is some good after all," Doggett declared challengingly.

"I guess it is," Jimson confessed. "I'd have steered clear of the subject if I'd known you were primed with all his dope."

"Well, it's all straight dope. Besides backing up the Legion post in its activities and rendering service to hospitalized veterans, the Auxiliary often does much good by giving help to the families of ex-service men in need. For instance, the Auxiliary in Mason City, Iowa, has a revolving fund of one thousand dollars. During the unemployment crisis it lent every cent of it to tide ex-service men over temporary

financial difficulties. I'll wager that, if one of us ran into hard luck and was actually down to rock bottom, you or I would a lot rather accept help from an ex-service organization than from some impersonal charity."

"Second the motion on that point," Jimson agreed.

"Now just to give you a concrete idea of the kind of work Auxiliary units do, I want to read you something my wife stuck in my pocket along with some other Auxiliary data."

Doggett fumbled in his pocket a moment and then drew out a slip of paper.

"Here it is. It's a report of the activities for one year of the Auxiliary unit attached to James R. Cutter Post of Abilene, Kansas. 'Participated in observance of Armistice Day, Flag Day, and Memorial Day; voted to equip and maintain a room in the new memorial hospital for ex-service men being erected at Abilene; had charge of local Salvation Army drive; assisted the Legion in two home-talent plays; conducted bazaars and food sales; sent a large box of magazines to hospital at Fort Riley; sold poppies on Memorial Day; contributed fifteen dollars to fund for decoration of overseas graves; sent clothing to Wichita Hospital; sent box of home-made jellies and jams to U. S.

P. H. S. hospital at Kansas City; sold one-hundred and seventy dollars' worth of helmets and poppies on Armistice Day; gave twenty-five dollars, nine Christmas boxes, and two bed lamps to Kansas City Hospital for the benefit of disabled soldiers. At the close of the year there was still a balance of two hundred dollars in the treasury.' That sounds to me like a good job well done."

"You win, old-timer," I said. "You've convinced me at least that an Auxiliary unit is a good investment, and I'm going back to recommend to my post that we start one as soon as possible."

"I'm glad you said that," Doggett replied, "because to tell the truth, I came to the convention with sailing orders from my skipper to spread all the propaganda I could about the Auxiliary. Now I can report progress to her. As for this old misogynist here—I think that's the fancy word for woman-hater —does he see the light yet?"

"Well, I'm weakening, anyhow," said Jimson.

"Good!" Doggett rose. "I've got to beat it now, fellows. See you tomorrow. As to the Auxiliary, just remember what I said before about wives. You can get along without one, but you can get along a lot better with one."

The Profiteer Hunt

(*Continued from page 6*)

Instead of agreeing to the payment to the company of $1,777,000, the Government has demanded of the Canadian Electro Products Company the return of the $1,750,000 advanced to build the plant, with interest at six percent. At this writing the sum totals about $2,500,000.

A distinguished New York lawyer retained by the A. E. P. has reminded the War Department of its "generally high and generous attitude" toward American contractors, a n d bespeaks similar treatment for a Canadian firm because Canada "bore the brunt of war for years before the United States entered it." We shall not offend the soldiers of heroic Canada by introducing them into this discussion; we shall merely suggest that the A. E. P. contract reveals how at least one Canadian-American war contractor "bore the brunt" of that war. The lawyer was on safe ground when he spoke of the "high and generous attitude" of our Government toward its own contractors. For example, let us see what the Duesenberg Motors Corporation did to bear the "brunt of war."

The Duesenberg Motors Corporation was incorporated in February of 1917. It acquired a plant in Elizabeth, New Jersey. The total investment was about $1,500,000. In November, 1917, it obtained a contract to manufacture five hundred Liberty motors. The Government agreed to pay all production costs plus a profit of $913.05 per motor, plus a bonus of twenty-five percent on manufacturing cost savings under $6,087 per motor. As the average cost of making a Liberty motor turned out to be about $3,000, this contract, excluding a fifteen percent profit on spare parts, would have netted the young Duesenberg company about $1,685 per motor, or $842,-500.

The extravagant nature of this con-

tract was recognized, and on December 11th it was amended. The fixed profit was reduced to $625 per motor and the "bogey" price under which a twenty-five percent bonus was to be paid was cut to $5,000. This would have saved the Government money, except for the inclusion of provisions whereby the Government bound itself to pay for the depreciation of the plant and for certain expensive tools, and to pay in full for heat-treating and inspecting operations, including buildings and equipment. The result was that these amendments, which were made for the ostensible purpose of protecting the Government, in reality opened the doors to increased profits for the contractor.

Three weeks later, on January 4, 1918, the contractor scored again. He won back nearly everything he had lost on December 11th, retained all he had gained, and multiplied the whole by four. The contract for 500 Liberty motors was amended to read 2,000 Bugatti motors, a French machine. The fixed profit per motor was jacked up from $625 to $750 and "bogey" boosted from $5,000 to $6,000. The twenty-five percent bonus was retained, as were also the stipulations of December 11th concerning depreciation, tools, heat-treating and inspection.

There were many other amendments from time to time, and every one of them is of a "high and generous" character, granting new favors to the contractor. One calls for an advance of $1,250,000 to the contractor, who gave his note—no mortgage. One advanced $400,000 more for the contractor to buy the F. I. A. T. plant at Poughkeepsie, New York, on which the depreciation is fixed in advance at $250,000. Thus the Duesenberg Motors Corporation got a $400,000 plant for $150,000. Another bound the Government to erect a permanent rather than temporary build-

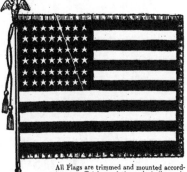

ings for inspection and heat-treating.
The Duesenberg's dealings with the
Government were wound up on August
14, 1919. Forty motors had been produced. They cost the government
$4,533,222. Two months later the
Duesenberg company sold out to the
Willys Corporation, automobile manufacturers. To give some idea of the
extent of the holdings of the Duesenberg company, which was started eighteen months before with $1,500,000 cash,
the Willys Corporation sold the F. I. A.
T. plant for $300,000, and the main
plant at Elizabeth, New Jersey, for
$5,525,000.

The Air Service auditors report illegal payments under the terms of the
August 14th settlement as follows:

Overhead expenses	$327,328
Depreciation	439,271
Profits	268,148
Rental of F. I. A. T. plant	25,479
Total	$1,060,226

A quick look at the "overhead" item
reveals some enlightening charges, all
of which were paid for by the Government as a part of the essential operation of manufacturing Bugatti motors.
There is a charge of $114,101 for
"value of marine and automobile parts
rendered obsolete by the war." These
parts had no relation whatsoever to the
government contract. They were used
in the company's civilian operations.
The company maintained a force of
plant guards for which the Government
paid $40,012. A smaller though no less
interesting charge is that of $81 for
box seats at automobile races. Traveling expenses totaled $30,000, of which
the auditors declare $11,000 were not
essential to the Government's contract.
The company's representatives enter-
tained royally, it seems. Numerous
"entertainment" items of from $50 to
$190 appear. The Government paid
$1,100 in taxes levied on one of the
company's subsidiary plants in Chicago
prior to our entrance into the war.
War taxes to the extent of several thousand dollars were charged to Uncle
Sam, as were directors' fees and the
maintenance expense of elaborate offices in Washington and New York.
Such items as these also appear:

Monogram for Dodge sedan	$5.00
Cigars	171.00
Expenses and freight on racing auto	20.58
Six boxes Mozart cigars for Traffic Dept.	15.00
Gratuity to freight handlers	30.00

The list could be extended. All such
payments are declared by the Air Service to be illegal. The Department of
Justice has acted in this case. A suit
of intervention has been filed to collect
$1,060,226.

Forty and Eight Campaign

THE chemins de fer of America are
going to hum this spring and summer as the Société des 40 Hommes et
8 Chevaux starts a membership excur-
sion campaign. Each of the five hundred voitures attached to posts in as
many towns and cities is expected to
make a night voyage to an adjoining
community to help organize a new voiture. Posts which have not yet organized a voiture may learn how to go
about it by writing H. E. McDonald,
Correspondant Nationale, 3122 Arcade
Bldg., Seattle, Wash.

uddy Can Pack Up His Troubles— But Naught Else

There were some things we learned in the service that will count against us until doomsday, or until the government medals are all given out. As an illustration of the above proverb, the art of rolling a pack stands out like the pocket flap on a rooky's shirt.

Manufacturers who make traveling bags, suitcases and trunks believe the ex-service persons roll their own equipment, same as in the slum era.

Picture Buddy and his family on the way to the railroad station in full pack. Think of the old Stave Hero swinging the family barracks bags to the top of a taxi or Little Buddy toting a hammock full of toys along the main street on moving day.

Manufacturers of this equipment must believe that in our homes are any of the goldfish boxes which we once appraised highly and in which was kept extra pairs of socks and cubical elephant tusk, hairbrushes, leaping dandruff powder, corn plasters, peanut bars, needle and thread, oil, sardines, shoe polish and liberty bonds.

Are they wrong?

Use the coupon for an answer. Roll the dots into an envelope and let's get some luggage. If we go into Frisco next fall with packs and barracks bags, they'll turn out the queerest looking guard we ever saw.

A Big Bertha envelope, containing 100 rounds of sales shrapnel, in other words 100 coupons, reached Buddy's barrel this week. This barrage was touched off by Comrade C. E. Mitchell, Commander Air Service Post 137, Cleveland, O. Notice how the heavy firing has lifted Ohio to the front. Here's the number of coupon rounds by sectors reaching the Stave Hero's intrenchments since Feb. 6, 1923:

Ohio	135	Wis.	27	Wash.	12	N. H.	3
Ky.	82	S. C.	25	Wyo.	10	Nev.	3
Ill.	80	Utah	24	Tenn.	11	Vt.	2
Minn.	75	Ind.	26	Me.	11	W. V.	2
Ia.	56	R. I.	18	Mo.	10	Ala.	1
Mass.	53	N. D.	16	Montana	9	Alaska	28
La.	38	Va.	16	N. C.	9	Dist. of Col.	3
Col.	31	La.	16	Miss.	8	France	2
Neb.	29	Texas	15	Okla.	8	Scotland	1
Iowa	28	S. D.	15	Ariz.	6	Belgium	1
Ore.	28	Mich.	14	Ark.	5	England	1
Kan.	27	Md.	13	Conn.	5	Spain	1
N. J.	26	Ga.	12	N. M.	4	Hawaii	2

There's cedar chests, too. We didn't need 'em over there as the seam chipmunks took care of the moths. But when buddy and sweetie trip over the matrimonial tentropes, they'll need a place to store the furs and other winter garments. And there's the Ligneous Legionnaire's army clothing in the corner of some closet and not a coot to challenge a moth advancing across No Man's Land. And those moths don't know a medal from a dog tag. A Croix de Guerre is dessert for them.

Sign the kupe, fold it up neatly and store it away in one of Uncle Sam's mailboxes. Later the manufacturers of cedar chests will get a squint at it and if they are satisfied that we use storage chests, perhaps they will join us.

What make of cedar chests do we want advertised in our columns.

Every reader a salesman, every salesman a buyer, every buyer a booster.

Clip and mail—ho!

United we boost; divided we bust.

To the Advertising Manager,
627 West 43d St., New York.

I would like to see the following make of trunks, cedar chests, traveling bags and suitcases advertised in our weekly:

....

....

Give reasons ....

....

This coupon is for all Legionnaires and Auxiliary Members to fill out.

But if you are a dealer or salesman, please check .... dealer.

Salesman. If not dealer or salesman, please state occupation ....

Name ....

Address ....

Post ....

LET'S PATRONIZE THEY ADVERTISE

THEY ADVERTISE LET'S PATRONIZE

We do not knowingly accept false or fraudulent advertising, or any advertising of an objectionable nature. See "Our Platform," issue of December 22, 1922. Readers are requested to report promptly any failure on the part of an advertiser to make good any representation contained in an advertisement in THE AMERICAN LEGION WEEKLY.

Advertising rates: $3.00 per agate line. Smallest copy accepted, 14 lines (1 inch). THE ADVERTISING MANAGER, 627 West 43d Street, N. Y. City.

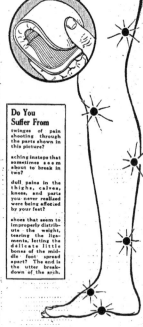